CAN'T COOK WON'T COOK
LEAVES HOME

Silvana Franco

This book is published to accompany the television series *Can't Cook Won't Cook*, produced by Bazal Midlands for BBC Birmingham.

Executive Producer: Trevor Hyett
Producer: Caroline Officer & Jill Francis
Director: Paul Colbert

Published by BBC Worldwide Ltd,
Woodlands, 80 Wood Lane, London W12 0TT

First published in 1998
Copyright © compilation Bazal 1998 (Bazal is a Broadcast Communications Plc Company)
Copyright © recipes Silvana Franco 1998
The moral right of the author has been asserted
Photographs by Paul Webster, copyright © BBC Worldwide Ltd 1998

ISBN 0 563 38423 9

Food Stylist: Silvana Franco
Commissioning Editor: Vivien Bowler
Editors: Jane Parsons and Kate Quarry
Art Directed by Ellen Wheeler
Design by Town Group Creative

Set in Compacta and Rotis SemiSans
Printed in Great Britain by Martins the Printers Ltd, Berwick-upon-Tweed
Bound in Great Britain by Hunter & Foulis Ltd, Edinburgh
Colour separation by Radstock Repro, Midsomer Norton
Cover printed by Belmont Press Limited, Northampton

Contents

Welcome

For most young people, the thought of cooking their own meals is one of the most daunting aspects of leaving the family home, but with *Can't Cook Won't Cook*'s help, easy, tasty and cheap meals are well within the most reluctant cook's grasp. These recipes have been written specifically for the new cook, they use the simplest techniques and include many short cuts to good results.

Follow each recipe exactly as it's written then, as you feel more confident with your new cookery skills, experiment and expand on the basic recipes. Most dishes are based around the evening meal, but some dishes are highlighted as being good for entertaining and there's a whole chapter on snacks. You'll also find useful guidelines for equipment, shopping and healthy eating, so let's rattle those pots and pans!

Eatingwell

It's incredibly important that you stick to regular, balanced meals when you begin cooking for yourself. If you don't eat properly your whole wellbeing will begin to suffer. The symptoms of an unhealthy diet include poor levels of concentration, tooth decay and a weakened immune system, meaning you catch every bug going round. A poor diet can also can also have a dramatic effect on your weight. The key to maintaining a healthy balance lies in eating a varied diet that ensures the intake of many different vitamins and minerals. Always eat when you are hungry, don't skip meals and don't fill up on snacks. Here's a quick check list to keep you on the right track:

- Eat a varied diet made up of three meals a day — don't skip breakfast

- Base your meals on carbohydrates such as rice, pasta, bread or potatoes

- Eat plenty of fresh fruit and vegetables

- Try to include some protein, such as meat, fish, cheese or eggs, with each meal

- Don't overdo the shop-bought snacks such as biscuits and chocolate

Healthandsafety inthekitchen

There's plenty of scope for trouble in a dangerous kitchen. Ensure that your kitchen is a safe place to be, and so avoid accidents and food poisoning:

Keep your kitchen clean
All surfaces, including the floor and all equipment, utensils and plates, should be kept clean. Don't let the washing-up pile up: wash up as you go along and always empty the bin as soon as it's full.

Store food correctly
Keep raw meats and cooked foods separate. Keep chilled foods chilled and dry goods dry. Don't ever risk eating food past its sell-by date.

Re-heating and defrosting
Only reheat food once. Don't re-freeze food that's already been frozen and don't ever rush-defrost food by, for example, thawing things in hot water or in the airing cupboard — all these things can lead to rapid bacteria multiplication and a good chance of food poisoning.

WON'T COOK

Gettingstarted

Kitchen Equipment

If you've just moved into your own home, it's important that you get things off on the right foot. The starting point is picking the right equipment to help your cooking to run smoothly.

When choosing your equipment go for the middle road in quality; there's no need to look at the top end of the market, but spending your cash on thin-based saucepans and flimsy utensils is a waste of money. A good place to visit is a catalogue shop where you can pick up all the equipment you need at a cut-rate price. Chances are, you'll be sharing accommodation with at least a couple of others, so each agree to buy specific items and pool your resources.

The recipes in this book call for little by way of specialist equipment; however, one item that's not included on the equipment shopping list is a hand-held blender and if you're going to get serious in the soup chapter, it's an invaluable piece of hardware that you'll be well advised to get hold of.

Here's a list of the basics:

two sizes of saucepan, with lids

frying pan

ovenproof casserole dish

small roasting tin

sturdy baking sheet

chopping board

two mixing bowls

can opener

cheese grater

rolling pin

measuring jug

kitchen scales

large metal sieve

balloon whisk

three wooden spoons

potato masher

garlic press

swivel-style vegetable peeler

slotted spoon

fish slice

pastry brush

large and small sharp knives

Stocking up

Student kitchens are notorious for their lack of cupboard space, so make sure you shop carefully. If you have useful items in stock such as rice and canned tuna, you'll always be able to knock up a decent meal. Write a list of what you need before you shop and stick to it — make sure you eat before you shop, or you'll end up with a basket full of chocolate and crisps.

Here's a list of items to get in stock before you start to cook:

Bottles and jars	Dried goods	Groceries
vegetable oil	plain flour	milk
olive oil	baking powder	eggs
vinegar	cornflour	butter
soy sauce	caster sugar	Cheddar
curry paste	spaghetti	Parmesan
chilli sauce	pasta shapes, e.g. penne	bread
mayonnaise	noodles	garlic
tomato ketchup	rice	onions
mustard	stock cubes	potatoes
	tomato purée	
Cans	mixed spices	
chopped tomatoes	dried mixed herbs	
baked beans		
tuna		

Fresh Parmesan is an essential element of most Italian-style pasta dishes. It is quite expensive, but really is worth splashing out on for the authentic flavour it brings to your cooking – and remember, a little goes a long way. Don't be tempted to plump for the dried varieties of Parmesan as they bear little resemblance to the real thing and will give your finished dish an unpleasant flavour.

Several of these recipes call for fresh herbs such as parsley or basil. Fresh herbs can really add a lovely flavour to your cooking but they will also push up your grocery bill, so one of the best ways to ensure a handy supply is to buy a small growing plant from a garden centre or supermarket and nurture it on a sunny windowsill. If your budget doesn't stretch that far, then skip fresh herbs altogether or use the dried alternative where indicated in the recipes.

Special extras

These are not essential items, but if you've just picked up your grant or are feeling a bit flush, they're very handy things to spend your cash on:

jar of pesto sauce

bottle of Worcestershire sauce

jar of Marmite

jar of peanut butter

jar of clear honey

jar of mango chutney

bag of dried red lentils

can of beans, e.g. kidney, cannellini

can of chick peas

dried chilli flakes

can of corned beef

Abouttherecipes

Here are a few notes about the recipes:

Metric and imperial quantities are given in the recipes but never mix them together as they are not interchangeable.

Sets of measuring spoons are available in both metric and imperial sizes to give accurate measurements of small quantities.

Spoon measures are level.

Medium eggs are used in the recipes unless otherwise specified.

snacks

Chillitortillas

Taco sauce can be bought in jars from most supermarkets, but if you can't find it, use 2 tablespoons of regular tomato relish and add a little water to the sauce.

 Preparation: 10 minutes | Cooking time: 15 minutes **Serves 2**

1 tablespoon sunflower oil

1 small onion, finely chopped

1 large garlic clove, finely chopped

225 g (8 oz) lean minced beef

100 g (4 oz) button mushrooms, sliced

¼ teaspoon dried chilli flakes or
hot chilli sauce

1 x 200 g (7 oz) can chopped tomatoes

1 x 200 g (7 oz) can kidney beans

6 tablespoons taco sauce

salt and pepper

To serve

4 flour tortillas

4 crisp lettuce leaves, shredded

1 x 150 ml (5 fl oz) carton soured cream
(optional)

1 Heat the oil in a large pan and cook the onion, garlic and mince for 2–3 minutes until beginning to brown. Add the mushrooms and dried chilli flakes or chilli sauce and cook for a further minute or so.

2 Stir in the chopped tomatoes, kidney beans and taco sauce and simmer gently for 10 minutes; season to taste.

3 Warm the tortillas in large, dry frying pan to soften them. Scatter the lettuce on each tortilla then spoon over the chilli; top with a dollop of soured cream, if using, then roll up and eat.

Nachos

Mexican bars and cinemas charge loads for a plate of nachos and yet they're so easy to make at home. Have a go yourself and taste the difference.

Preparation: 5 minutes | Cooking time: 5 minutes **Serves 2**

1 x 150 g (5 oz) bag tortilla chips
1 x 200 g (7 oz) can chopped tomatoes
4 salad onions, thinly sliced
2 mild fresh red chillies, thinly sliced
50 g (2 oz) Gruyère or Cheddar, grated
salt and pepper

1 Pre-heat the grill to medium.

2 Tip the tortilla chips into a large flameproof dish. Spoon over the chopped tomatoes and season lightly. Scatter over the salad onions, chillies and, finally, the cheese.

3 Place under the grill for 5 minutes until heated through; serve warm.

Crispyonionrings

This is a great snack from Can't Cook Won't Cook *presenter Ainsley Harriott. He says that the longer you leave the onions soaking, the better the result.*

Preparation: 10—35 minutes | Cooking time: 5 minutes **Serves 2**

1 Spanish onion
150 ml (5 fl oz) milk
6 tablespoons flour, seasoned with salt and pepper
vegetable oil, for frying

1 Slice the onion into 1 cm (½ in) wide slices, then separate the rings. Place in a bowl with the milk and set aside for 5—30 minutes.

2 Heat 5 cm (2 in) of vegetable oil in a deep frying pan.

3 Drain the onion rings, dust in the seasoned flour, then fry in batches for 2—3 minutes until crisp and golden brown. Drain on kitchen paper and eat hot.

Greek-style lambkebabs

Give the local kebab shop a miss on your way back from the pub and knock up your own truly tasty skewers with all the trimmings – in no time at all.

 Preparation: 10 minutes | Cooking time: 15 minutes **Serves 2**

250 g (9 oz) lean lamb cubes

1 tablespoon olive oil

1 teaspoon ground mixed spice

¹/₄ teaspoon salt

¹/₄ teaspoon caster sugar

1 onion, cut into wedges

salt and pepper

For the yoghurt dressing

1 x 200 g (7 oz) carton Greek-style yoghurt

a pinch of caster sugar

1 garlic clove, crushed

juice of ¹/₂ a lemon

pitta bread and salad, to serve

1 Place the lamb cubes in a bowl and add the olive oil, spice, salt, sugar and plenty of pepper; rub the mixture into the flesh.

2 Pre-heat the grill to high. Thread the spiced lamb cubes and onion wedges on to four skewers. Drizzle over a little more oil and cook under the grill for 12–15 minutes, turning occasionally, until charred and tender.

3 Make the dressing: stir together the yoghurt, sugar, garlic and lemon juice and season well to taste. Drizzle the dressing over the kebabs and serve with pitta and salad.

TIP

Add texture to the yoghurt dressing by stirring in a little diced cucumber or red onion.

Irishrarebit

This is a fantastic post-pub snack and the best bit is that you get to drink the rest of the bottle of Guinness with your rarebit.

 Preparation: 5 minutes | Cooking time: 5 minutes **Serves 1**

50 g (2 oz) Irish Cheddar, finely grated

1 teaspoon English mustard

a small knob of butter

1 tablespoon Guinness

2 teaspoons Worcestershire sauce

2 thick slices of bread

1 Mix together the cheese, mustard, butter, Guinness and Worcestershire sauce until well blended.

2 Toast the bread on one side, then spread the cheese mixture on the uncooked side. Place back under the grill for 2—3 minutes until bubbling.

Salmonmega-burgers

This clever recipe can be made using any firm-fleshed fish such as cod or monkfish, but is particularly good with salmon which, despite its posh image, is not much more expensive than cod. Serve the burgers with French fries and garlic mayonnaise for a very smart supper.

 Preparation: 10 minutes | Cooking time: 5 minutes **Serves 2**

300 g (10 oz) salmon tail fillet, skinned and boned

1 tablespoon Dijon mustard

2 tablespoons flour, seasoned with salt and pepper

1 tablespoon olive oil

a small knob of butter

salt and pepper

1 lemon, cut into wedges, to serve

1 Place the salmon on a chopping board and chop finely using a heavy knife. Mix with the mustard and plenty of seasoning.

2 Using wet hands, shape the mixture into two even-sized cakes. Dust with the seasoned flour.

3 Heat the oil and butter in a small frying pan and cook the salmon burgers for 2—3 minutes on each side until golden but still pink in the centre.

4 Drain on kitchen paper and serve with lemon wedges.

WON'T
COOK

Ainsley's crispy sweetcorn fritters

These are one of Ainsley's favourite snacks. They're crispy and chewy at the same time and any left-overs can be eaten cold.

Preparation: 5 minutes | Cooking time: 10 minutes Serves 4

1 x 420 g (14 ¾ oz) can creamed sweetcorn

1 salad onion, finely chopped

4—5 heaped tablespoons cornflour

vegetable oil, for frying

salt and pepper

1 Mix together the corn, salad onion, cornflour and plenty of seasoning.

2 Heat a little oil in large frying pan and cook large spoonfuls of the mixture for 3—4 minutes on each side until crisp and golden.

3 Drain on kitchen paper and serve.

Hash browns

The starch in the potato keeps this mixture together when it's fried but it also makes grating it a bit of a sticky business. The finished result is so crisp and moreish, it's well worth getting your hands a bit messy.

Preparation: 5 minutes | Cooking time: 25 minutes Serves 2

2 small floury potatoes

vegetable oil, for frying

salt and pepper

1 Cook the whole potatoes in a pan of boiling, salted water for 15 minutes until just tender. Drain and cool slightly.

2 Coarsely grate the potatoes into a bowl and season generously. Firmly shape the mixture into four oval patties by patting the mixture together in the palms of your hands.

3 Heat a little oil in a large frying pan and cook the patties for 3—4 minutes on each side until crisp and golden. Drain on kitchen paper and serve hot.

Chips

There really is nothing worse than a soggy chip with a hard centre. Here's how to make sure yours turn out crisp.

 Preparation: 10 minutes | Cooking time: 6–10 minutes **Serves 1**

1 large potato

vegetable oil, for frying

cubes of bread, to test oil temperature

salt

1 Scrub the potato in cold water and cut into fingers as thick or thin as you choose. Wash well to rinse off the excess starch and prevent them sticking together during cooking. Dry thoroughly with kitchen paper.

2 Heat 5 cm (2 in) of vegetable oil in a small, deep frying pan. Test the oil temperature with a cube of bread — it should not be too hot at this stage and the bread should take 60 seconds to turn brown. When the oil has reached the right temperature, cook the chips for 5 minutes or until pale golden.

3 Remove with a slotted spoon and drain on kitchen paper. Raise the heat slightly and when the oil is hot enough to brown a cube of bread in 30 seconds, return the chips to the pan for 1–2 minutes until crisp and golden. Drain on kitchen paper, sprinkle with salt and eat hot.

Japanesechickenwings

Forget boring old barbecue-style chicken wings — these are a modern, teriyaki-inspired version.

 Preparation: 5 minutes, plus extra for marinating | Cooking time: 20 minutes **Serves 2**

4 tablespoons dark soy sauce

4 tablespoons dry sherry

1 tablespoon clear honey

12 chicken wings

1 Mix together the soy sauce, sherry and honey. Add the chicken wings and leave to marinate (20 minutes–12 hours).

2 Pre-heat the grill to medium.

3 Arrange the chicken wings on the grill pan and cook under the grill for 20 minutes, turning occasionally, until cooked through and crisp-skinned.

WON'T
COOK

Glamorgan sausages ⓥ

This classic vegetarian dish is very tasty. Where possible choose a crumbly textured cheese such as Caerphilly or Wensleydale although any full-flavoured cheese will do.

 Preparation: 10 minutes | Cooking time: 10 minutes **Serves 2**

50 g (2 oz) fresh white breadcrumbs

100 g (4 oz) cheese, finely grated

1 small leek, finely chopped

2 tablespoons chopped fresh parsley

¼ teaspoon dried mixed herbs

1 tablespoon wholegrain or Dijon mustard

1 egg, beaten

1–2 tablespoons plain flour

vegetable oil, for frying

salt and pepper

spaghetti hoops or baked beans, to serve

1 Mix together the breadcrumbs, cheese, leek, parsley, dried herbs, mustard, egg and plenty of seasoning. Using damp hands, shape the mixture into four sausage shapes. Dust lightly with flour.

2 Heat 1 cm (½ in) of vegetable oil in a large frying pan and cook the sausages for 6–8 minutes, turning occasionally until crunchy and golden. Drain on kitchen paper and serve hot with spaghetti hoops or baked beans.

TIP

Try making these with a bunch of salad onions in place of the leek.

Hotstickyribs

Make these as hot as you like by adding more or less chilli sauce. They can be finished off very successfully on a barbecue.

 Preparation: 5 minutes | Cooking time: 30 minutes   **Serves 2**

6 pork ribs, weighing 300 g (11 oz) in total

2 tablespoons clear honey

2 tablespoons malt vinegar

1—2 tablespoons hot chilli sauce

1 Cook the ribs in a pan of boiling water for 15 minutes, then drain well.

2 Pre-heat the grill to medium. Mix together the honey, vinegar and hot chilli sauce and rub over the ribs.

3 Arrange on the grill pan and cook for 15 minutes, turning and basting occasionally until well browned. Serve hot.

Brilliantbeefburgers

A classic beefburger is an almost unbeatable snack, and these are really quick to make — perfect for food on the run.

 Preparation: 5 minutes | Cooking time: 10 minutes   **Serves 2**

250 g (9 oz) lean beef mince

1 tablespoon finely chopped gherkins

vegetable oil, for frying

salt and pepper

burger buns, shredded lettuce and mustard, to serve

1 In a large bowl, mix together the mince, gherkins and plenty of salt and pepper. Shape the mixture into two even-sized patties.

2 Heat a little oil in a large frying pan and cook the burgers for 4—5 minutes on each side until well browned but still a little pink in the centre.

3 Serve in burger buns with plenty of shredded lettuce and a squirt of mustard.

WON'T
COOK

Friedcheese

Okay, so it's not the healthiest of snacks, but it's so irresistibly oozy — just don't eat it every day.

 Preparation: 5 minutes | Cooking time: 5 minutes **Serves 2**

1 egg

1 garlic clove, crushed

vegetable oil, for frying

225 g (8 oz) cheese such as Mozzarella or Cheddar, cut into 2 cm (3/4 in) cubes

2 tablespoons flour, seasoned with salt and pepper

salt and pepper

1 Beat together the egg, garlic and seasoning.

2 Heat 2.5 cm (1 in) of vegetable oil in a deep frying pan.

3 Dust the cheese cubes in the seasoned flour, dip them in the beaten egg mixture, then cook for 2 minutes, turning occasionally, until crisp and golden. Drain on kitchen paper and eat immediately.

Spicypopcorn

Bags of popcorn are really poor value for money. Save cash by making your own and enjoy it freshly popped and still warm.

Preparation: 5 minutes | Cooking time: 5 minutes **Serves 2**

1 tablespoon vegetable oil

1/2 teaspoon salt

2 tablespoons popcorn kernels

1 garlic clove, crushed

1 fresh red chilli, seeded and very finely chopped

1 tablespoon freshly grated Parmesan

1 Heat the oil in a large pan and add the salt and popcorn. As it starts to pop, throw in the garlic and chilli, cover with a lid and cook for 2—3 minutes, until the corn has stopped popping.

2 Sprinkle over the Parmesan, shake the pan, then turn out into a bowl and eat warm.

Vegetable pakora

Use whatever vegetable you choose, but don't mix them together — if you want to use a selection of vegetables, make up individual batches of mixture.

 Preparation: 5 minutes | Cooking time: 5 minutes **Serves 2**

50 g (2 oz) self-raising flour

1/4 teaspoon ground turmeric

1/2 fresh red chilli, finely chopped

1/4 teaspoon salt

75 g (3 oz) roughly chopped vegetable such as onion, cauliflower, spinach, broccoli or courgette

vegetable oil, for frying

mango chutney, to serve

1 Place the flour, turmeric, chilli and salt in a bowl. Add enough water to form a very thick batter. Stir in the chopped vegetable.

2 Heat 5 cm (2 in) of oil in a deep frying pan and drop in tablespoonsful of the mixture. Cook for 4—5 minutes, turning occasionally, until golden brown and cooked through.

3 Drain on kitchen paper and serve warm with mango chutney.

Melting banana sarnie

A real treat for eggy-bread fans, this gooey sandwich makes a fantastic breakfast following a heavy night.

Preparation: 10 minutes | Cooking time: 10 minutes **Serves 1**

1 small, ripe banana

2 slices of white bread

4 squares of milk chocolate

1 egg

1 teaspoon caster sugar

2 tablespoons milk

a large knob of butter

1 Mash the banana with a fork and spread thickly on to a slice of the bread. Place the chocolate squares on top of the banana, top with the other slice and press down firmly to make a sandwich.

2 Beat the egg, sugar and milk together in a shallow dish and put the sandwich into the mixture. Press down with a spatula and set aside for a few minutes, turning occasionally until the bread absorbs all the liquid.

3 Gently heat the butter in a small frying pan and cook the sandwich for 3—4 minutes on each side until puffed and golden.

WON'T COOK

pasta

Zesty chicken and broccoli pasta

Vary the green vegetables used in this recipe and try it with sugar-snap peas, mangetout, frozen peas or fine green beans.

 Preparation: 5 minutes | Cooking time: 15 minutes **Serves 2**

175 g (6 oz) dried rigatoni

1 large skinless, boneless chicken breast, cut widthways into 1 cm (¹/₂ in) wide strips

grated rind and juice of 1 lime or ¹/₂ lemon

2 tablespoons olive oil

1 garlic clove, finely chopped

175 g (6 oz) broccoli, broken into small florets

1 x 150 ml (5 fl oz) carton double cream

salt and pepper

freshly grated Parmesan, to serve

1 Cook the pasta in a large pan of boiling, salted water according to packet instructions.

2 Meanwhile, place the chicken strips in a bowl with the citrus rind, olive oil and garlic; season well and mix together.

3 Heat a small frying pan and when very hot, cook the chicken pieces for 3 minutes on each side until cooked through and golden brown.

4 Add the broccoli to the pan of cooking pasta 3—4 minutes before it is ready.

5 Squeeze the lemon or lime juice over the chicken, stir in the cream and season well.

6 Drain the pasta and broccoli, then and return to the pan. Pour over the creamy chicken sauce and toss well together. Divide between two serving bowls, sprinkle over plenty of Parmesan and serve.

TIP

Vary this dish by using soft cheese such as mascarpone in place of the double cream – but don't try it with single cream as the citrus juice will curdle the sauce.

WON'T
COOK

Spaghetti with fresh pesto sauce Ⓥ

Fresh pesto can easily be adapted to suit the ingredients you have in stock. Try a combination of fresh herbs such as parsley, coriander, dill or tarragon, or substitute the pine nuts for natural-roasted peanuts, pistachios or blanched almonds.

 Preparation: 5 minutes | Cooking time: 15 minutes **Serves 2**

225 g (8 oz) dried spaghetti

1 large growing basil plant or
2 x 15 g (½ oz) packs

2 tablespoons pine nuts

2 garlic cloves

2 tablespoons olive oil

50 g (2 oz) butter, at room temperature

50 g (2 oz) freshly grated Parmesan, plus extra to serve

salt and pepper

1 Cook the pasta in a large pan of boiling, salted water according to packet instructions.

2 Using a heavy knife, finely chop together the basil, pine nuts and garlic cloves until the mixture forms a coarse paste. Place the mixture in a small bowl and stir in the oil, butter, Parmesan and plenty of seasoning.

3 Spoon 4 tablespoons of the pasta cooking water into the pesto mixture, then drain the pasta well. Return the pasta to the pan and stir in the pesto mixture.

4 Divide between two serving bowls, sprinkle over a little more Parmesan and serve.

Mixed mushroom and bacon spirals

Mushrooms and bacon are a lovely flavour combination, but if you feel like pushing the boat out, swap the lemon juice and olive oil for a small carton of double cream.

 Preparation: 5 minutes | Cooking time: 10 minutes **Serves 2**

175 g (6 oz) dried pasta spirals

a large knob of butter

4 rashers smoked streaky bacon, roughly chopped

1 garlic clove, roughly chopped

200 g (7 oz) mixed mushrooms such as chestnut, field mushrooms and button, sliced

1 tablespoon fresh lemon juice

2 tablespoons olive oil

2 tablespoons chopped fresh parsley

salt and pepper

freshly grated Parmesan, to serve

1 Cook the pasta in a large pan of boiling, salted water according to packet instructions.

2 Meanwhile, heat the butter in a large frying pan and stir-fry the bacon and garlic for 1–2 minutes. Add the mushrooms and continue to cook for a further 2–3 minutes until golden; season to taste.

3 Drain the pasta, then return to the pan. Stir in the mushroom mixture, lemon juice, olive oil and parsley and toss well together. Divide between two serving bowls, scatter over some freshly grated Parmesan and serve.

TIP

Choose sturdy varieties of mushroom and avoid the fancy, delicate types such as oyster. Besides being very expensive, they break down very quickly and don't have a full enough flavour for this dish.

WON'T
COOK

Spaghetti with infused oil (V)

*This is a very simple yet really tasty dish that needs little preparation.
It should be served straight, so don't be tempted to sprinkle over any Parmesan.*

 Preparation: 5 minutes | Cooking time: 10 minutes **Serves 2**

150 g (5 oz) dried spaghetti

4 garlic cloves

2 fresh red birds'-eye chillies

6 tablespoons olive oil

4 tablespoons chopped fresh coriander or parsley

salt and pepper

1 Cook the pasta in a large pan of boiling, salted water according to packet instructions.

2 Meanwhile, slice the garlic cloves thickly. Halve the chillies lengthways and scrape out the seeds. Cut widthways into thin strips.

3 Place the olive oil, garlic and chilli into a small pan and heat very gently without colouring; continue to keep warm until the spaghetti is ready.

4 Spoon 4 tablespoons of the pasta cooking water into the oil mixture, then drain the pasta well.

5 Return the pasta to the pan and pour over the chilli oil mixture. Add the chopped herbs and toss well together; check the seasoning.

6 Divide the pasta between two bowls, grind over plenty of black pepper and serve immediately.

TIP

Birds'-eye chillies are very hot, so please take care when handling them. Always use a knife to scrape out the seeds, which you should then discard. Wash your hands and utensils thoroughly after handling and avoid touching sensitive areas such as the eyes or lips. The widely available jalapeño chilli is quite a bit milder than the birds'-eye and makes a good alternative for those who wish to lower the heat a little.

Spaghetti Bolognese

Although traditionally made with beef, other minced meats such as lamb, pork or even sausagemeat can be used for this dish.

 Preparation: 10 minutes | Cooking time: 25 minutes **Serves 2**

2 tablespoons olive oil

1 small onion, chopped

1 carrot, chopped

1 garlic clove, finely chopped

2 rashers smoked streaky bacon, chopped

225 g (8 oz) lean minced beef

1 x 400 g (14 oz) can chopped tomatoes

1 teaspoon honey or sugar

1 tablespoon Worcestershire sauce

175 g (6 oz) dried spaghetti

a few drops of Tabasco

salt and pepper

freshly grated Parmesan, to serve

1 Heat the oil in a pan and cook the onion, carrot, garlic and bacon for 5 minutes until softened. Add the mince and cook for a further 5 minutes until browned. Stir in the chopped tomatoes, honey and Worcestershire sauce and simmer for 10—15 minutes.

2 Meanwhile, cook the pasta in a large pan of boiling, salted water according to packet instructions.

3 Stir a few drops of Tabasco into the sauce and season to taste.

4 Drain the pasta, then return to the pan. Pour in the sauce, toss well together and divide between two bowls. Sprinkle over plenty of Parmesan and serve immediately.

WON'T COOK

Crusty lamb lasagne

Avoid ready-made supermarket lasagnes — they're soggy, dull and expensive. Make your own, however, and you're in for a satisfying and flavour-packed supper that's ready to serve in less than an hour.

 Preparation: 10 minutes | Cooking time: 30 minutes **Serves 2**

1 tablespoon olive oil

1 small onion, finely chopped

1 small aubergine, cut into 1 cm (1/2 in) dice

250 g (9 oz) lean minced lamb

1 x 200 g (7 oz) can chopped tomatoes

2 tablespoons tomato ketchup

100 g (4 oz) dried lasagne

150 g (5 oz) mature Cheddar, grated

1 tablespoon freshly grated Parmesan

salt and pepper

leafy green salad, to serve

1 Pre-heat the oven to 220°C/425°F/Gas 7.

2 Heat the oil in a large pan and cook the onion, aubergine and lamb for 5 minutes until beginning to brown. Stir in the chopped tomatoes and ketchup and simmer gently for 10 minutes; season to taste.

3 Arrange a layer of lasagne in the base of a small ovenproof dish and spoon over one-third of the lamb mixture. Scatter over a handful of Cheddar and repeat the layers twice, finishing with the remaining Cheddar.

4 Sprinkle the Parmesan over the top and bake the lasagne in the oven for 15—20 minutes until the pasta is cooked through and the top is bubbling and crusty. Serve with plenty of green salad.

TIP

Buy the dried lasagne that needs no pre-cooking.

Pastashellswith spicysausagesauce

Choose good-quality sausages such as Cumberland or Lincolnshire from your local butcher or the fresh meat counter of a supermarket rather than opting for the cheaper, often unpleasant-tasting, pre-packed varieties — it will make a real difference to your finished dish.

 Preparation: 10 minutes | Cooking time: 15 minutes **Serves 2**

250 g (9 oz) spicy pork sausages, cut into 1 cm (1/2 in) pieces

1 yellow pepper, seeded and cut into thin strips

2 garlic cloves, thinly sliced

175 g (6 oz) dried pasta shells

1 x 400 g (14 oz) can chopped tomatoes

1 tablespoon soy sauce

50 g (2 oz) frozen peas, thawed

salt and pepper

For the crunchy topping

1 tablespoon olive oil

50 g (2 oz) fresh white breadcrumbs

1 tablespoon freshly grated Parmesan

1 Heat a large frying pan and cook the sausage pieces for 1—2 minutes. Add the pepper strips and garlic and cook for 2—3 minutes until beginning to soften.

2 Cook the pasta in a large pan of boiling, salted water according to packet instructions.

3 Stir the chopped tomatoes and soy sauce into the sausage pan and simmer gently for 5—6 minutes.

4 Make the topping: heat the olive oil in a small pan and stir-fry the breadcrumbs for 3—4 minutes until golden brown. Stir in the Parmesan and remove from the heat.

5 Stir the peas into the sausage pan and cook for a couple of minutes until tender; season to taste.

6 Drain the pasta, then return to the pan. Stir in the sausage sauce, mix well and divide between two large bowls. Sprinkle over the crunchy topping and serve immediately,

WON'T
COOK

Pasta with tuna and peas

The chilli adds a little kick to this speedy pasta dish — if you don't have any to hand, use a pinch of dried chilli flakes or good shake of Tabasco.

 Preparation: 10 minutes | Cooking time: 20 minutes **Serves 2**

225 g (8 oz) dried pasta shapes

1 tablespoon olive oil

1 onion, chopped

1 garlic clove, sliced

1 fresh red chilli, seeded and finely chopped

1 x 200 g (7 oz) can tuna in oil, drained

150 g (5 oz) frozen peas, thawed

1 tablespoon mayonnaise

2 tablespoons chopped fresh parsley

salt and pepper

1 Cook the pasta in a large pan of boiling, salted water according to packet instructions.

2 Meanwhile, heat the oil in a pan and cook the onion, garlic and chilli for 5 minutes until softened. Add the tuna and 100 ml (3½ fl oz) of water and cook gently for 6—8 minutes or until the pasta is cooked. Stir in the peas, mayonnaise and parsley and season to taste.

3 Drain the pasta, then return to the pan. Tip in the sauce and toss well together. Divide between two bowls and serve with a good grinding of black pepper.

Tagliatelle with nutty olive salsa Ⓥ

Save time by preparing double quantities of this versatile salsa and storing it in the fridge for up to five days. It's not only great with pasta but can be put to lots of other good uses — try spreading it on bread when making sandwiches, mixing it with crème fraîche and serving as a dip or stirring it into creamy mashed potato for a tasty accompaniment.

 Preparation: 5 minutes | Cooking time: 15 minutes **Serves 2**

175 g (6 oz) dried tagliatelle

50 g (2 oz) pitted black olives

25 g (1 oz) salted peanuts

1 large garlic clove

3 tablespoons chopped fresh basil or parsley

2 tablespoons olive oil

1 tablespoon fresh lemon juice

2 tablespoons freshly grated Parmesan, plus extra to serve

salt and pepper

1 Cook the pasta in a large pan of boiling, salted water according to packet instructions.

2 Make the salsa: place the olives, nuts and garlic on a large board and chop with a heavy knife until the mixture forms a coarse paste. Place in a bowl and stir in the herbs, olive oil, lemon juice and Parmesan; season to taste.

3 Drain the pasta, then return to the pan. Stir in the sauce and toss well together. Divide between two bowls and serve with an extra sprinkling of Parmesan.

TIP

Use mild black olives for this dish as the full-flavoured varieties may be a little overpowering.

Pepperandpestopenne

Red pesto adds plenty of flavour to this quick dish — if you don't have any in stock, use a squirt of tomato purée and a handful of chopped fresh herbs such as parsley or basil.

Preparation: 5–10 minutes | Cooking time: 20 minutes **Serves 2**

3 tablespoons olive oil

2 red peppers, seeded and cut into 1 cm (1/2 in) strips

175 g (6 oz) dried penne

2 ripe tomatoes

2 tablespoons red pesto

salt and pepper

freshly grated Parmesan, to serve

1 Heat the olive oil in a large pan and cook the peppers over a medium heat for 15 minutes until softened and golden. Season to taste.

2 Meanwhile, cook the pasta in a pan of boiling salted water according to packet instructions.

3 Roughly chop the tomatoes. When the peppers are cooked, stir the tomatoes, pesto and 2 tablespoons of water into the pan; cook for 1–2 minutes until the tomatoes are warmed through. Season to taste.

4 Drain the pasta well, then return to the pan. Add the red pepper mixture and toss well together. Divide between two serving bowls, sprinkle over the Parmesan and serve.

Cheat'smacaronicheese

A tasty macaroni cheese is a marvellous thing, and this speedy recipe is foolproof.

Preparation: 5 minutes | Cooking time: 10 minutes **Serves 2**

225 g (8 oz) dried macaroni

1 x 200 g (7 oz) carton soft cheese

4 tablespoons milk

1 tablespoon wholegrain mustard

175 g (6 oz) mature Cheddar, grated

salt and pepper

1 Cook the pasta in a large pan of boiling, salted water according to packet instructions.

2 Meanwhile, gently heat the soft cheese, milk, mustard and three-quarters of the grated cheese in a small pan, stirring until the mixture melts; do not allow it to boil. Season with a little salt and plenty of pepper.

3 Pre-heat the grill to high. Drain the pasta, then return to the pan. Pour in the sauce and mix well, then transfer to a flameproof dish, scatter over the remaining cheese and cook under the grill for 2–3 minutes until golden and bubbling.

CAN'T
COOK

RigatoniFiorentina

This little number contains spinach and cheese, which is typical of food from Florence — hence its name.

 Preparation: 5 minutes | Cooking time: 15 minutes **Serves 2**

175 g (6 oz) dried rigatoni

1 tablespoon olive oil

1 garlic clove, crushed

200 g (7 oz) fresh spinach

1 x 200 g (7 oz) can chopped tomatoes

1 x 150 g (5 oz) ball Mozzarella, drained and cubed

2 tablespoons freshly grated Parmesan

salt and pepper

1 Cook the pasta in a large pan of boiling, salted water according to packet instructions.

2 Heat the oil in a wok or large frying pan and stir-fry the garlic and spinach over a high heat for 2 minutes, stirring until the spinach wilts. Stir in the chopped tomatoes; season to taste and simmer together for 3–4 minutes.

3 Drain the pasta, then return to the pan. Pre-heat the grill to high. Stir in the spinach mixture, then transfer to a flameproof dish. Push the Mozzarella cubes into the pasta, leaving them quite near the surface, then sprinkle over the Parmesan. Flash under the grill for 2–3 minutes until the cheese bubbles. Serve hot.

Spaghetticarbonara

This Italian classic is so easy that even the most reluctant of student cooks will meet the grade.

 Preparation: 5 minutes | Cooking time: 15 minutes **Serves 2**

225 g (8 oz) dried spaghetti

a knob of butter

1 small onion, chopped

2 garlic cloves, finely chopped

6 rashers smoked streaky bacon, chopped

2 eggs, beaten

1 x 150 ml (5 fl oz) carton single cream

2 tablespoons freshly grated Parmesan, plus extra to serve

salt and pepper

1 Cook the pasta in a large pan of boiling, salted water according to packet instructions.

2 Meanwhile heat the butter in a small frying pan and cook the onion, garlic and bacon for 5 minutes until golden.

3 Beat together the eggs, cream, Parmesan and plenty of seasoning.

4 Drain the pasta well, then return to the pan. Stir in the bacon mixture and the cream mixture and toss well together. Divide between two bowls, sprinkle over a little extra Parmesan and a good grinding of black pepper and serve.

WON'T COOK

Stir-fried hammy pasta

This dish uses the wafer-thin style of ham, but you could make it with regular ham cut into small strips. Penne or spiral shapes would work well.

 Preparation: 5 minutes | Cooking time: 15 minutes **Serves 2**

175 g (6 oz) dried pasta shapes

1 tablespoon olive oil

1 garlic clove, finely chopped

1 courgette, cut into matchsticks

100 g (4 oz) wafer-thin smoked ham, roughly shredded

1 teaspoon wholegrain mustard

50 g (2 oz) Cheddar, grated

salt and pepper

1 Cook the pasta in a large pan of boiling, salted water according to packet instructions. Drain well.

2 Heat the oil in a wok or large frying pan and stir-fry the garlic, courgette sticks and ham for 2—3 minutes until golden brown. Add the pasta and stir-fry for a further 2 minutes.

3 Stir in the mustard and cheese and cook for a further minute or so until the cheese melts; season to taste and serve immediately.

Creamy vodka pasta ⓥ

Pierce three or four hot red chillies with a fork and place in a quarter bottle of vodka. Leave to infuse for at least a week then — hey presto! — your own home-made chilli vodka for half the price of the designer versions.

 Preparation: 5 minutes | Cooking time: 15 minutes **Serves 2**

225 g (8 oz) dried spaghetti

a small knob of butter

2 plum tomatoes, roughly chopped

1 garlic clove, finely chopped

4 tablespoons chilli vodka

1 x 150 ml (5 fl oz) carton double cream

salt and pepper

freshly grated Parmesan, to serve

1 Cook the spaghetti in a large pan of boiling, salted water according to packet instructions.

2 Heat the butter in a small pan and gently cook the tomatoes and garlic for 3 minutes. Add the vodka to the tomato pan and boil rapidly for 2 minutes. Lower the heat and continue to simmer for a further 2—3 minutes. Stir in the carton of cream and simmer gently for 5 minutes; season to taste.

3 Drain the pasta, then return to the pan. Pour in the cream sauce and mix well together. Transfer the spaghetti to two bowls and sprinkle over plenty of Parmesan and black pepper.

Above: Greek-style lamb kebabs (page 12)   **Below:** Salmon mega-burgers (page 13)

Below: Roast tomato soup (page 35)   Above: Minestrone soup (page 43)

Above: Pepper and pesto penne (page 30)   Below: Creamy vodka pasta (page 32)

Below: Fu Manchu fried rice (page 65)   Above: Chicken balti (page 82)

Above: Bacon bubble and squeak (page 48)   Below: Baking-tray tomato tarts (page 57)

Below: King prawn chow mein (page 70)   Above: Tropical noodles (page 67)

red roast lamb (page 88) · sweet chick pea stew (page 76)

Below: Gin and lime froth (page 90)   Above: Bitter choc pots (page 90)

soups

Mushroom soup ⓥ

This is a very thick, luxurious-tasting soup. It can be thinned down with vegetable stock, if you prefer. Small bottles of sherry are widely available quite cheaply from supermarkets or off licences, but as an alternative you can use port, Madeira, Marsala or even a fruity red wine.

 Preparation: 10 minutes | Cooking time: 15 minutes **Serves 2**

a large knob of butter

1 small onion, finely chopped

2 garlic cloves, finely chopped

200 g (7 oz) chestnut mushrooms, finely diced

100 ml (3½ fl oz) medium sherry

1 tablespoon flour

300 ml (10 fl oz) milk

1 x 150 ml (5 fl oz) carton double cream

4 tablespoons chopped fresh parsley

salt and pepper

hot buttered toast, to serve

1 Heat half the butter in a large pan and cook the onion and garlic for 5 minutes until they are beginning to turn golden.

2 Meanwhile, heat the remaining butter in a frying pan and cook the mushrooms for 3—4 minutes until softened. Stir in the sherry and bubble rapidly for 2 minutes.

3 Stir the flour into the onion pan and cook for 1 minute, then gradually add the milk. Bring to the boil, stirring until the mixture is smooth and thickened. Stir in the mushroom mixture and cook gently for 5 minutes.

4 Stir in the cream and parsley, season to taste and cook for a further 2—3 minutes until piping hot, but not boiling. Stir in the parsley, ladle into bowls and serve with hot buttered toast.

Roasttomatosoup

This is a really easy way to make soup, and the garlic and tomatoes develop a delicious roasted flavour.

Preparation: 5 minutes | Cooking time: 45 minutes **Serves 2**

8 tomatoes

4 garlic cloves

1–2 tablespoons olive oil

1 tablespoon brown sugar

600 ml (1 pint) hot vegetable or chicken stock

4 tablespoons chopped fresh coriander or parsley

salt and pepper

crusty bread, to serve

1 Pre-heat the oven to 220°C/450°F/Gas 7. Halve the tomatoes and arrange in a roasting tin, cut-side up.

2 Nestle the whole garlic cloves between the tomatoes. Season well with salt and pepper, then drizzle over the olive oil. Sprinkle with sugar and roast for 30 minutes until the tomatoes are softened and a little charred.

3 Pour over the hot stock and return to the oven for 15 minutes. Blend the mixture using a hand-held blender.

4 Stir in the chopped herbs and season to taste. Pour into two bowls and serve with crusty bread.

Easylentilsoup

This delicious and substantial soup is really economical to make.

Preparation: 10 minutes | Cooking time: 35 minutes **Serves 2**

1 tablespoon olive oil

2 garlic cloves, finely chopped

1 small onion, finely chopped

1 large carrot, finely diced

2 tomatoes, roughly diced

50 g (2 oz) red lentils

600 ml (1 pint) vegetable stock

juice of 1/2 lemon

salt and pepper

1 Heat the oil in a large pan and cook the garlic, onion and carrot for 3–4 minutes until beginning to soften.

2 Add the tomatoes, lentils and stock, bring to the boil, cover and simmer gently for 30 minutes.

3 Season the soup to taste, stir in the lemon juice and serve.

WON'T
COOK

Orangepepper soupwithcroutons ⓥ

The tasty, cheesy croutons add the finishing touch to a colourful dinner-party first course.

 Preparation: 10 minutes | Cooking time: 35 minutes **Serves 2**

1 tablespoon olive oil

2 carrots, diced

1 onion, chopped

1 leek, thinly sliced

2 orange peppers, seeded and diced

250 g (9 oz) potatoes, diced

600 ml (1 pint) vegetable stock

salt and pepper

For the croutons

2 thick slices of bread, crusts removed

1 tablespoon olive oil

1 tablespoon freshly grated Parmesan

1 Pre-heat the oven to 220°C/425°F/Gas 7. Heat the oil in a large pan and cook the carrots, onion and leek for 5 minutes until softened.

2 Add the peppers, potatoes and stock and bring to the boil. Cover and simmer for 30 minutes until the vegetables are softened.

3 Meanwhile, cut the bread into cubes and place in a large bowl, drizzle over the oil and Parmesan and toss well together. Arrange on a baking sheet and cook in the oven for 10 minutes, turning occasionally until crisp and golden.

4 Push the soup through a sieve or liquidize with a hand-held blender, then return to the pan. Heat through and season to taste. Divide between bowls and garnish with croutons.

SpeedyFrenchonion soupwithcheesecroûtes

A traditional French onion soup takes hours to make, yet this one has a very developed flavour with less than 30 minutes of cooking.

 Preparation: 5 minutes | Cooking time: 25 minutes **Serves 2**

50 g (2 oz) butter

3 large Spanish onions, sliced

1 tablespoon caster sugar

150 ml (5 fl oz) dry white wine

600 ml (1 pint) hot chicken or vegetable stock

1 tablespoon Worcestershire sauce

2 garlic cloves, crushed

2 tablespoons mayonnaise

1 mini baguette

a few drops of Tabasco or chilli sauce

100 g (4 oz) Gruyère or Cheddar, grated

1 tablespoon brandy (optional)

salt and pepper

1 Melt the butter in a large pan, add the onions, sprinkle over the sugar and cook over a high heat for 5—10 minutes, stirring frequently, until well browned.

2 Pour the wine into the pan and cook vigorously for 1—2 minutes. Stir in the hot stock and Worcestershire sauce, bring to the boil and simmer for 10–15 minutes until the onions are tender.

3 Meanwhile, mix together the crushed garlic and mayonnaise. Pre-heat the grill to high. Diagonally slice the baguette and toast under the grill for 1—2 minutes on each side. Shake a few drops of Tabasco or chilli sauce on to the toast, then pile the cheese on top. Return to the grill and cook for 1—2 minutes until bubbling and golden.

4 Stir the brandy, if using, into the soup, season to taste, then, using a slotted spoon, divide the onions between two soup bowls. Place the cheese croûtes on top of the onions, then ladle over the hot soup. Top with a spoonful of the garlic mayonnaise and serve.

TIP

Ready-made garlic mayonnaise is available in supermarkets.

Smokypea andbaconsoup

Canned yellow split peas can be found in most supermarkets.

 Preparation: 5 minutes | Cooking time: 25 minutes **Serves 2**

1 tablespoon vegetable oil

1 small onion, finely chopped

2 garlic cloves, finely chopped

8 rashers smoked streaky bacon, finely chopped

1 x 400 g (14 oz) can yellow split peas, drained

600 ml (1 pint) hot chicken stock

2 tablespoons freshly grated Parmesan

salt and pepper

crusty bread, to serve

1 Heat the oil in a large pan and cook the onion, garlic and bacon for 5 minutes until beginning to soften.

2 Add the split peas and stock and bring to the boil, then cover and simmer for 15—20 minutes until the peas are completely softened.

3 Season to taste and ladle into bowls. Sprinkle over the Parmesan and a good grinding of black pepper and serve with the bread.

TIP

You can buy a whole bag of dried yellow split peas for roughly the same price as a can of cooked yellow split peas. For this recipe, soak 75 g (3 oz) dried peas overnight then cook according to the packet instructions. Drain well and use as for the canned.

Crab and sweetcorn soup

This is a really authentic-tasting Chinese-style soup that also works very well using cooked chicken in place of the crab sticks. For a more substantial dish, cook 50 g (2 oz) rice noodles in boiling water, then place in the bottom of the serving bowls; ladle over the hot soup and serve.

 Preparation: 10 minutes | Cooking time: 15 minutes **Serves 2**

1 tablespoon vegetable oil

1 garlic clove, finely chopped

1 cm (½ in) piece root ginger, finely chopped

1 tablespoon cornflour

600 ml (1 pint) hot chicken stock

1 x 230 g (8¼ oz) can sweetcorn, drained

6 crab sticks, roughly chopped

1 egg

1 tablespoon fresh lemon juice

1 teaspoon soy sauce

salt and pepper

50 g (2 oz) bag prawn crackers, to serve

1 Heat the oil in a deep pan and gently cook the garlic and ginger for 2—3 minutes without colouring.

2 Blend the cornflour with a little stock and add to the soup pan with the remaining stock, sweetcorn and crab. Bring to the boil, stirring continuously, and simmer gently for 3—4 minutes.

3 Beat together the egg, lemon juice and soy sauce and slowly trickle into the soup pan, stirring slowly with a chopstick or fork to make egg strands. Season to taste and serve with prawn crackers.

Chicken and rice soup

This recipe calls for risotto rice, but ordinary pudding rice can be substituted.

 Preparation: 10 minutes | Cooking time: 20 minutes **Serves 2**

1 tablespoon vegetable oil

1 x 100 g (4 oz) boneless, skinless chicken breast, roughly chopped

2.5 cm (1 in) piece root ginger, finely chopped

2 garlic cloves, finely chopped

2 fresh red chillies, seeded and finely chopped

50 g (2 oz) medium-grain or risotto rice

600 ml (1 pint) hot chicken stock

2 tablespoons freshly grated Parmesan

salt and pepper

1 Heat the oil in a large pan and cook the chicken, ginger, garlic and chillies for 3—4 minutes, stirring frequently until golden.

2 Stir in the rice and stock, bring to the boil, cover and simmer gently for 15 minutes until the rice is tender.

3 Season to taste, stir in the Parmesan, then ladle into bowls and serve.

TIP

A teaspoon of Thai red curry paste can be used in place of the ginger, garlic and chillies – just stir it in with the stock.

Creamy cornchowder

The mashed potato used in this chowder gives the finished soup a wonderful velvety texture.

Preparation: 15 minutes | Cooking time: 25 minutes **Serves 3—4**

600 ml (1 pint) milk

1 vegetable stock cube

450 g (1 lb) potatoes, diced

1 tablespoon olive oil

1 small onion, finely chopped

1 garlic clove, finely chopped

2 fresh red chillies, seeded and finely chopped

¼ teaspoon dried thyme

1 x 510 g (1lb 2½oz) can sweetcorn, drained

1 x 200 g (7 oz) carton crème fraîche

salt and pepper

1 Place the milk, stock cube and diced potatoes in a pan and heat gently for 15 minutes until the potato is tender.

2 Meanwhile, heat the oil in a large pan and cook the onion, garlic, chillies and thyme for 3—4 minutes until softened but not browned.

3 Roughly mash the potato into the milk, then stir in the onion mixture and sweetcorn. Simmer for 3—4 minutes, then stir in the crème fraîche, season to taste and serve.

WON'T
COOK

Creamycarrotsoup Ⓥ

The pairing of caramelized onions and naturally sweet carrots makes a delicious flavour combination. Sprinkle over a few fresh basil leaves for a smart dinner-party starter.

 Preparation: 15 minutes | Cooking time: 35 minutes **Serves 2**

a large knob of butter

1 Spanish onion, sliced

3 large carrots, diced

1 teaspoon sugar

450 ml (15 fl oz) vegetable stock

1 x 150 ml (5 fl oz) carton double cream

2 tablespoons chopped fresh parsley

salt and pepper

buttered granary rolls, to serve

1 Heat the butter in a pan and cook the onion for 6–8 minutes, stirring frequently until golden brown. Add the carrots and sugar and cook for a further 5 minutes.

2 Pour over the stock, bring to the boil, cover and simmer for 20 minutes until the carrots are tender. Purée the soup with a hand-held blender, then stir in the cream and heat through.

3 Stir in the parsley, season to taste and serve with buttered granary rolls.

Minestrone soup (V)

Choose any type of small pasta for this dish, or snap spaghetti or tagliatelle into small lengths.

 Preparation: 15 minutes | Cooking time: 20 minutes **Serves 2**

50 g (2 oz) tiny pasta shapes

1 tablespoon olive oil

1 small onion, chopped

1 garlic clove, chopped

1 carrot, diced

1 small potato, diced

1 small leek, diced

2 tomatoes, diced

1 tablespoon tomato purée

600 ml (1 pint) hot vegetable stock

2 tablespoons pesto

1 tablespoon freshly grated Parmesan

salt and pepper

1 Cook the pasta in a large pan of boiling, salted water according to packet instructions. Drain well.

2 Meanwhile, heat the olive oil in a large pan and cook the onion, garlic, carrot, potato and leek for 5 minutes. Add the tomatoes, tomato purée and stock, cover and simmer for 10–15 minutes until the vegetables are tender.

3 Stir in the cooked pasta and the pesto sauce; season to taste. Ladle into bowls, sprinkle with Parmesan and serve.

TIP

If you're in a hurry, cut down on preparation time by using a bag of frozen, diced vegetables.

WON'T
COOK

Kevin'schunky chickensoup

This tasty country-style soup comes courtesy of Can't Cook Won't Cook *presenter Kevin Woodford.*

 Preparation: 10 minutes | Cooking time: 20 minutes **Serves 2**

25 g (1 oz) butter

1 small onion, finely chopped

1 x 100 g (4 oz) boneless chicken breast, diced

1 garlic clove, finely chopped

1 large leek, thinly sliced

1 large potato, diced

600 ml (1 pint) hot chicken stock

2 tablespoons chopped fresh parsley

juice of ½ lemon

salt and pepper

crusty bread, to serve

1 Heat the butter in a large pan and cook the onion and chicken for 2 minutes. Stir in the garlic, leek and potato and cook gently for a further 5 minutes.

2 Pour in the stock, bring to the boil and simmer for 15 minutes until the chicken and vegetables are cooked.

3 Season to taste and stir in the parsley and lemon juice. Ladle into bowls and serve with bread.

Bluecheesesoup (V)

This may sound a little strange, but it's a must for all blue-cheese fans. And any left-overs cool to make a smooth paste that can be spread on bread and grilled Welsh rarebit-style for a delicious snack.

 Preparation: 10 minutes | Cooking time: 10 minutes **Serves 2**

a small knob of butter

1 garlic clove, crushed

1 tablespoon cornflour

300 ml (10 fl oz) milk

300 ml (10 fl oz) vegetable stock

225 g (8 oz) Dolcelatte, crumbled

225 g (8 oz) Gruyère, grated

salt and pepper

French bread, to serve

1 Heat the butter in a small pan and gently cook the garlic for 2 minutes until softened but not coloured.

2 Blend the cornflour with a little of the milk, then pour into the pan with the remaining milk and the stock. Bring to the boil, stirring until the mixture thickens.

3 Add the cheeses and cook gently, stirring until the cheese dissolves. Season to taste, then ladle into bowls and serve with bread.

TIP

If you can't get hold of Dolcelatte, use any type of mild blue cheese such as Cambazola or Cashel Blue for this dish.

WON'T
COOK

Curried
pumpkinsoup Ⓥ

Choose any squash for this soup: pumpkin, acorn squash or butternut squash, which has a lovely nutty flavour, are all good choices.

 Preparation: 10 minutes | Cooking time: 40 minutes **Serves 2**

1 tablespoon olive oil

1 small onion, finely chopped

450 g (1 lb) finely diced pumpkin

450 ml (15 fl oz) hot vegetable stock

2 tablespoons curry paste

1 x 150 ml (5 fl oz) carton single cream

2 tablespoons chopped fresh coriander

salt and pepper

warm naan bread, to serve

1 Heat the oil in a large pan and cook the onion and pumpkin over a gentle heat for 5 minutes until beginning to turn golden. Pour over the hot stock, stir in the curry paste, cover and simmer for 30 minutes until tender.

2 Liquidize with a hand-held blender or push the mixture through a sieve. Return to the pan, stir in the cream and heat through gently, without boiling.

3 Stir in the coriander and season to taste. Ladle into bowls and serve with warm naan bread.

potatoes and pastries

Bacon bubble and squeak

The ideal left-overs dish. You can use any cooked potatoes, such as roasties, in a bubble and squeak and most greens work well, too — try Brussels, spinach or broccoli, or follow this recipe and cook the lot from scratch.

 Preparation: 15 minutes | Cooking time: 20 minutes **Serves 2**

350 g (12 oz) floury potatoes, diced

½ small Savoy cabbage, shredded

2 tablespoons vegetable oil

6 rashers smoked streaky bacon, cut widthways into strips

1 small onion, chopped

2 garlic cloves, crushed

2 fresh red chillies, seeded and thinly sliced

2 teaspoons Worcestershire or soy sauce

salt and pepper

baked beans or spaghetti hoops, to serve

1 Cook the potatoes in a large pan of boiling, salted water for 8 minutes. Add the cabbage and cook for a further 3—4 minutes until tender.

2 Meanwhile, heat the oil in a large frying pan and cook the bacon, onion, garlic and chillies for 5 minutes until golden.

3 Drain the potatoes and cabbage well and add to the frying pan. Crush with a wooden spoon and then leave the mixture to cook over a medium heat for 2—3 minutes until a crust forms on the bottom.

4 Break up the mixture, stir in the Worcestershire sauce, season to taste, then leave to cook again until a crust forms on the bottom, then break up and cook for a third time. Spoon on to plates and serve with baked beans or spaghetti hoops.

Vegetarian cottage pie Ⓥ

This is a really tasty dish — the mango chutney certainly makes the filling sparkle, but any kind of relish, pickle or chutney can be used or, failing that, try a dollop of brown sauce or ketchup.

 Preparation: 10 minutes | Cooking time: 15 minutes **Serves 2**

500 g (1 lb 2 oz) potatoes, cubed

1 tablespoon vegetable oil

1 small carrot, diced

1 small onion, finely chopped

1 garlic clove, finely chopped

100 g (4 oz) dried red lentils

300 ml (10 fl oz) hot vegetable stock

1 tomato, diced

2 teaspoons Worcestershire sauce

1 tablespoon milk

a small knob of butter

25 g (1 oz) frozen peas, thawed

1 tablespoon mango chutney

50 g (2 oz) mature Cheddar, grated

salt and pepper

1 Cook the potatoes in a large pan of boiling, salted water for 10–12 minutes until tender.

2 Heat the oil in a large pan and cook the carrot, onion and garlic for 1–2 minutes. Add the lentils and stock, bring to the boil and cook rapidly for 5 minutes.

3 Pre-heat the grill to high. Stir the tomato and Worcestershire sauce into the lentil pan and simmer gently for 3–4 minutes until tender.

4 Drain the potatoes well and mash with the milk, butter and seasoning.

5 Stir the peas and mango chutney into the lentils and cook for a further minute or so; season to taste and spoon into a flameproof dish. Spoon the mashed potato on top, scatter over the cheese and place under the hot grill for 1–2 minutes until golden.

Cheeseandhampasties

These pasties puff up brilliantly in the oven. You could vary the fillings to suit your store-cupboard – try baked beans, bacon and eggs.

 Preparation: 10 minutes | Cooking time: 15 minutes **Serves 4**

1 x 375 g (13 oz) pack ready-rolled puff pastry

2 tablespoons Dijon or wholegrain mustard

200 g (7 oz) ham

150 g (5 oz) Cheddar, grated

2 tablespoons milk

baked beans or spaghetti hoops, to serve

1 Pre-heat the oven to 220°C/450°F/Gas 7. Open out the pastry and cut into quarters to give four 20 x 11 cm (8 x 4½ in) rectangles.

2 Spread the pastry with mustard, then lay the ham on one half and sprinkle over the cheese. Fold each rectangle in half then, using a fork, press down around the edges to seal.

3 Brush the tops with milk and bake for 12–15 minutes until puffed and golden brown. Serve with baked beans or spaghetti hoops.

Cornedbeefhashcakes

Corned beef's a great thing to keep in store — it mashes up brilliantly for hash and, when paired with English mustard, makes the best sandwiches.

 Preparation: 10 minutes | Cooking time: 20 minutes **Serves 2**

350 g (12 oz) floury potatoes, diced

2–3 tablespoons vegetable oil

1 small onion, chopped

2 garlic cloves, crushed

1 x 200 g (7 oz) can corned beef

flour for dusting

salt and pepper

baked beans or spaghetti hoops, to serve

1 Cook the potatoes in a large pan of boiling, salted water for 10–12 minutes until tender.

2 Meanwhile, heat 1 tablespoon of oil in a small frying pan and cook the onion and garlic for 5 minutes until softened.

3 Chop the corned beef roughly and place in a bowl; stir in the onion mixture.

4 Drain the potatoes and add to the corned beef mixture. Crush with a fork, stirring to combine the mixture. Season to taste and shape into four cakes.

5 Heat 1–2 tablespoons of oil in a large frying pan. Dust the cakes with a little flour and cook over a high heat for 2 minutes on each side until golden. Serve with baked beans or spaghetti hoops.

CAN'T
COOK

Classicshepherd'spie

Add variety to this staple by cooking other vegetables with the potatoes and then mashing them up to make a mixed mash topping — try it with sweet potatoes, carrots, celeriac or parsnips.

 Preparation: 10 minutes | Cooking time: 15 minutes **Serves 2–3**

450 g (1 lb) floury potatoes, diced

1 tablespoon vegetable oil

1 small onion, finely chopped

1 large carrot, diced

300 g (10 oz) minced lamb

300 ml (10 fl oz) hot lamb stock

1 tablespoon tomato ketchup

2 teaspoons soy sauce

2 tablespoons milk

a knob of butter

1 teaspoon cornflour

75 g (3 oz) frozen peas, thawed

a few drops of Tabasco

salt and pepper

1 Cook the potatoes in a large pan of boiling, salted water for 10–12 minutes until tender.

2 Meanwhile, heat the oil in a large frying pan and cook the onion and carrot for 1 minute, then add the lamb mince and stir-fry until well browned. Pour in the hot stock and stir in the tomato ketchup and soy sauce. Bring to the boil and simmer rapidly for 3–4 minutes.

3 Drain the potatoes well and return to the pan, mash well, then beat in the milk and butter until smooth and creamy.

4 Mix the cornflour with a little water and add to the lamb mixture with the peas; bring back to the boil, stirring until slightly thickened. Season with salt, pepper and Tabasco to taste.

5 Pre-heat the grill to medium. Spoon the mince mixture into a flameproof dish and top with the mashed potato. Using a fork, mark a criss-cross pattern on the top.

6 Place under the grill for 3 minutes until the pie is speckled with brown.

WON'T
COOK

PorkandStiltonslice

What a versatile dish — have it hot for your supper, cold for your packed lunch or make mini ones and have a party!

 Preparation: 10 minutes | Cooking time: 30 minutes **Serves 2**

250 g (9 oz) sausagemeat

4 tablespoons Branston pickle

1 x 375 g (13 oz) pack ready-rolled puff pastry

50 g (2 oz) Stilton

2 tablespoons milk

baked beans, to serve

1 Pre-heat the oven to 200°C/400°F/Gas 6. Place the sausagemeat in a bowl and break up with a table knife. Spoon in the pickle and mix well with the knife.

2 Open out the pastry, place the sausage mixture lengthways across the centre, then crumble over the Stilton. Dampen the edges of the pastry with a little of the milk and fold over to enclose the filling.

3 Turn over the roll so the join is underneath, then seal the ends of the roll by firmly pressing the pastry together with your fingertips.

4 Transfer to a baking sheet, brush with milk and slash the surface with a small knife. Bake for 25–30 minutes until the pastry is risen and dark golden and the sausagemeat is cooked through.

5 Cut the pastry roll into slices and serve with baked beans.

Newpotatotortilla Ⓥ

A tortilla is a thick, Spanish-style potato omelette. This version is more of a Greek-inspired dish as it is made with feta cheese. Serve any leftovers cold with salad or top with mayonnaise and sandwich between bread for a smashing pack-up.

 Preparation: 5 minutes | Cooking time: 20 minutes **Serves 2**

200 g (7 oz) new potatoes, thinly sliced

5 eggs

1 garlic clove, thinly sliced

4 salad onions, finely chopped

1/2 teaspoon dried rosemary

1 tablespoon olive oil

50 g (2 oz) feta or Cheddar

salt and pepper

mixed salad, to serve

1 Thinly slice the potatoes and cook in a large pan of boiling, salted water for 5 minutes until just tender.

2 Meanwhile, crack the eggs into a large bowl and beat well together. Stir in the garlic, salad onions and rosemary with plenty of seasoning.

3 Heat the oil in 20 cm (8 in) frying pan. Drain the potatoes well and stir into the egg mixture. Pour into the hot pan and cook for 1 minute or so, stirring until the egg begins to set.

4 Break the feta into small pieces or dice the Cheddar and scatter over the top of the tortilla. Cook for 4 minutes until the egg is almost completely set.

5 Pre-heat the grill to medium. Place the pan under the pre-heated grill for 2—3 minutes until golden brown. Serve with salad.

TIP

Tortillas are very adaptable. It's a good idea to keep potatoes as a base but you can add just about any other vegetable such as sliced red pepper or leftover cooked broccoli. If you don't have any potatoes, use a couple of handfuls of fresh white breadcrumbs and you'll have an Italian-style frittata instead.

WON'T
COOK

Tunafishcakes

Canned tuna is used here, but canned salmon or poached fresh cod can be substituted very successfully.

 Preparation: 10 minutes | Cooking time: 20 minutes **Serves 2**

350 g (12 oz) floury potatoes, diced

1 tablespoon mayonnaise

1 x 85 g (3¼ oz) can tuna in oil, drained

2 tablespoons chopped fresh coriander or parsley

1 bunch of salad onions, finely chopped

1 garlic clove, crushed

2 tablespoons flour

1 egg, beaten

8 tablespoons dried natural breadcrumbs

vegetable oil for frying

salt and pepper

baked beans or mixed salad, to serve

1 Cook the potatoes in boiling, salted water for 10–15 minutes until tender. Drain well, return to the pan and mash together with the mayonnaise.

2 Meanwhile, flake the tuna and stir into the mash with the coriander, salad onions and garlic; season well to taste.

3 Shape the mixture into four even-sized patties. Dust lightly with flour, then dip into the beaten egg and then the breadcrumbs.

4 Heat a little oil in a frying pan and gently cook the fish cakes for 3–4 minutes on each side until crisp and golden; drain on kitchen paper. Serve with baked beans or salad.

TIP

Dried natural breadcrumbs can be bought in boxes from supermarkets. If you prefer, make your own by grating a couple of slices of day-old white bread.

Potato calzone ⓥ

This recipe uses that fantastic fresh bread dough that comes in a twist-open cardboard tube. If you can't get hold of it, use a packet of dried bread mix and make up the dough according to the packet instructions. It's a real carbo-loaded dish, so it's ideal if you're in need of energy.

 Preparation: 10 minutes | Cooking time: 30 minutes **Serves 2**

250 g (9 oz) floury potatoes, diced

1 x 300 g (11 oz) tube of fresh bread dough or petit pain dough

1 tablespoon plain flour

a knob of butter

4 salad onions, finely chopped

4 tablespoons milk

50 g (2 oz) Cheddar, grated

salt and pepper

salad, to serve

1 Pre-heat the oven to 220°C/450°F/Gas 7. Cook the potatoes in a large pan of boiling, salted water until tender.

2 Cut the dough in half, then, using floured hands, pat each piece out into a 15 cm (6 in) round.

3 Heat the butter in a small pan and gently cook the onions for 2 minutes until beginning to soften. Add half the milk, warm gently and remove from the heat.

4 Drain the potatoes, then return to the pan. Mash well, then add the cheese and salad onion mixture, stirring until the cheese melts; season to taste and allow to cool a little.

5 Divide the mixture between the circles of bread dough, then fold over, pressing the edges together to enclose the filling. Brush with the remaining milk, place on a baking sheet and cook for 12–15 minutes until the dough is golden brown and cooked through. Serve hot with lots of salad.

Cheesyfrying-panpizza

This really does work brilliantly – the base is like a scone mixture rather than a bread dough, so it doesn't need to be left to rise for ages, and because you load it with toppings while it's already cooking in the pan, it takes no time at all to cook through. If you're really in a hurry, you can always use a ready-made tomato sauce.

 Preparation: 10 minutes | Cooking time: 25 minutes **Serves 2**

3 tablespoons olive oil

1 garlic clove, finely chopped

1 small onion, finely chopped

1 x 200 g (7 oz) can chopped tomatoes

2 tablespoons tomato ketchup

225 g (8 oz) self-raising flour

25 g (1 oz) mature Cheddar, grated

150 ml (5 fl oz) warm water

toppings of your choice, e.g. sliced mushrooms, olives, salami, cheese

salt and pepper

coleslaw or salad, to serve

1 Make the sauce: heat 1 tablespoon of olive oil in a small pan and gently cook the garlic and onion for 5 minutes until softened. Stir in the tomatoes and ketchup and simmer gently for 10 minutes; season to taste.

2 Meanwhile, stir together the flour, cheese and a pinch of salt, make a well in the centre and pour in the warm water. Bring together to make a soft dough, then pat or roll out to a 20 cm (8 in) round.

3 Heat 1 tablespoon of oil in a large frying pan. Cook the dough for 6–7 minutes until the underside is golden. While the base is cooking, spoon over the tomato sauce, then scatter over your choice of toppings. Season to taste.

4 Pre-heat the grill to medium. Drizzle the remaining oil over the pizza and place under the grill for 3–4 minutes until bubbling and golden. Serve hot with plenty of coleslaw or salad.

Creamypotatolayer

This is based on the classic French dish, pommes dauphinoise, *of which there are many different versions. This version contains smoked bacon and can be served with baked beans, roast tomatoes or lots of salad for a delicious supper. The cooking time is affected by the thickness of the potato slices, so insert a knife into the centre to test that they are cooked through before serving.*

 Preparation: 15 minutes | Cooking time: 45 minutes **Serves 2**

a knob of butter
500 g (1lb 2 oz) potatoes, very thinly sliced
1 small onion, finely chopped
2 garlic cloves, finely chopped
2 tablespoons freshly grated Parmesan
8 rashers smoked streaky bacon, chopped
150 ml (5 fl oz) double cream
salt and pepper

1 Pre-heat the oven to 200°C/400°F/Gas 6.

2 Generously butter a deep, heatproof casserole dish. Arrange a layer of potatoes in the dish, then scatter over a little chopped onion, garlic, Parmesan, bacon and a small spoonful of the cream; season generously. Continue to layer, finishing with a covering of potato.

3 Dot the top with a little butter, sprinkle over some Parmesan, then bake for 45 minutes until cooked through and golden brown.

Baking-traytomatotarts ⓥ

Ready-rolled sheets of puff pastry are a great invention — you don't even need a rolling pin to produce these stylish tarts.

 Preparation: 10 minutes | Cooking time: 15 minutes **Serves 4**

1 x 375 g (13 oz) pack ready-rolled puff pastry
2 tablespoons red pesto or black olive paste
300 g (11 oz) mixed tomatoes, e.g. cherry, plum
1 x 150 g (5 oz) ball Mozzarella, drained and sliced
salt and pepper
mixed salad leaves, to serve

1 Pre-heat the oven to 220°C/425°F/Gas 7.

2 Open out the pastry, and cut into quarters to give four 20 x 11 cm (8 x 4 in) rectangles. Place on a large baking sheet. Using a small, sharp knife, score a 1cm (½ in) border around the edge of each rectangle.

3 Spread the pesto or olive paste over the pastry, making sure the mixture stays within the border. Roughly quarter or slice the tomatoes and casually arrange on top of the pesto. Top with the Mozzarella.

4 Season well and bake for 15 minutes until puffed and golden. Serve with salad.

 WON'T COOK

57

Smoked haddock tart

Ready-made pastry cases are available in the bakery section of large supermarkets.

 Preparation: 10 minutes | Cooking time: 10 minutes **Serves 2–3**

150 ml (5 fl oz) milk

250 g (9 oz) smoked haddock tail

25 g (1 oz) butter

1 onion, finely chopped

25 g (1 oz) plain flour

150 ml (5 fl oz) double cream

1 egg, beaten

2 tablespoons chopped fresh parsley

1 x 20 cm (8 in) ready-made shortcrust pastry case

2 tablespoons grated Cheddar

salt and pepper

salad or steamed vegetables, to serve

1 Place the milk in a large frying pan and heat gently. Add the fish and simmer gently for 4–5 minutes until cooked through.

2 Meanwhile, heat the butter in a separate pan and cook the onion for 2 minutes. Stir in the flour and cook for 1 minute, then remove from the heat.

3 Using a fish slice, carefully lift the cooked haddock on to a plate. Strain the milk a little at a time into the flour mixture, beating well until smooth. Stir in the cream and egg and bring to the boil, stirring until thickened. Season with black pepper and simmer very gently for 1–2 minutes.

4 Pre-heat the grill to medium. Remove the skin from the fish and discard. Flake the flesh into large chunks, gently mix with the parsley and cream sauce; spoon into the pastry case. Sprinkle over the cheese and place under the grill for 1–2 minutes until bubbling and golden brown.

5 Cut into wedges and serve with salad or vegetables.

Baked potatoes (V)

Thick-skinned potatoes such as Maris Piper or King Edwards make the best baking potatoes as they have a great, floury, fluffy texture when cooked — avoid using the small new potatoes both for baking and making mash as their texture is too firm and waxy. If you prefer your baked potato to have a very crunchy skin, leave it in the oven for an extra 20 minutes or, for a softer skin, rub a little olive oil into the surface before cooking.

 Preparation: 5 minutes | Cooking time: 1 hour **Serves 1**

1 x 250 g (9 oz) potato

a knob of butter

salt and pepper

1 Pre-heat the oven to 200°C/400°F/Gas 6. Scrub the potato in clean, cold water and pat dry.

2 Pierce the potato a few times with a fork to prevent it splitting open during cooking. Place directly on to the oven shelf and bake for 1 hour until soft when squeezed.

3 Cut open and serve with a large knob of butter and plenty of salt and pepper.

Fillings

Roast tomato and pesto
Quarter a couple of tomatoes and roast with the potato. Cut a cross in the top of the baked potato and squeeze it open, drop in a dollop of red pesto and top with the roasted tomatoes and a sprinkling of chopped salad onions.

Curried beans and cheese
Cook some chopped onion and garlic in a little vegetable oil until golden. Stir in a can of baked beans and a tablespoon of curry paste and gently heat through. Spoon into a hot, buttered baked potato and sprinkle over a handful of grated Cheddar.

Garlic and cheese mayo
Tuck some whole garlic cloves around the potatoes and roast for 30 minutes. Pop the garlic out of their skins, mash to a purée, then mix with mayonnaise and grated cheese. Pile into a hot buttered baked potato and serve hot.

Refried beans
Cook some chopped onion, garlic and chilli until golden. Add a small can of red kidney beans and a small can of chopped tomatoes and roughly mash together with a potato masher. Season to taste and pile into a hot buttered potato.

WON'T COOK

noodles and rice

Paella

True paella always contains saffron, but it's really expensive, so in order to get the authentic colour — although not quite the same flavour — this recipe uses ground turmeric. You can buy freshly cooked seafood cocktail from large supermarkets. It usually contains steamed squid, mussels and prawns, and has no dressing.

 Preparation: 15 minutes | Cooking time: 30 minutes **Serves 2**

1 tablespoon vegetable oil

1 small onion, chopped

1 garlic clove, chopped

2 x 150 g (5 oz) chicken drumsticks

1/2 teaspoon ground turmeric

600 ml (1 pint) hot chicken stock

175 g (6 oz) medium-grain or risotto rice

2 tomatoes, roughly chopped

100 g (4 oz) ready-prepared seafood cocktail

50 g (2 oz) frozen peas, thawed

1 tablespoon chopped fresh parsley

juice of 1 lime or 1/2 lemon

salt and pepper

1 Heat the oil in a large pan and cook the onion, garlic and chicken for 5 minutes until beginning to brown. Stir in the turmeric and cook for a further minute, then add the stock. Cover and simmer for 10 minutes.

2 Add the rice and tomatoes and cook, covered, for 15 minutes, stirring regularly until the grains are tender.

3 Stir in the seafood and peas and cook for a further 3—4 minutes until piping hot. Stir in the parsley and lime or lemon juice; season to taste and serve.

Oven-baked lemon-chilli chicken

This takes longer to cook than most of the other recipes in this book, but is quick to prepare and once it's in the oven, you can get back to your revision.

 Preparation: 10 minutes | Cooking time: 40 minutes **Serves 2**

225 g (8 oz) long-grain rice

juice and grated rind of 1 lemon

1 garlic clove, finely chopped

1/2 teaspoon dried chilli flakes

4 x 100 g (4 oz) skinless chicken thighs

a small knob of butter

1 lemon, thinly sliced

750 ml (1 1/4 pints) chicken stock

salt and pepper

1 Pre-heat the oven to 180°C/350°F/Gas 4. Place the rice, lemon rind, garlic, chilli flakes and plenty of salt and pepper in a large ovenproof dish or roasting tin and mix well together.

2 Place the chicken on top of the rice mixture, dot with the butter and season. Arrange the lemon slices on top of the chicken.

3 Mix together the lemon juice and stock and pour over the chicken. Bake for 40 minutes until the chicken is cooked through and the rice is tender.

Cajunrice

The spice in this dish comes from a ready-made blend of seasonings packaged as Cajun spice. If you can't get it, use dried or fresh red chillies and perhaps a squeeze of fresh lemon juice to give your dish a bit of a kick.

 Preparation: 10 minutes | Cooking time: 25 minutes **Serves 2**

1 tablespoon vegetable oil

1 small onion

2 garlic cloves, finely chopped

1 red pepper, seeded and diced

2 teaspoons Cajun seasoning

125 g (4½ oz) long-grain white rice

100 g (4 oz) chorizo or other cured sausage, roughly diced

75 g (3 oz) cooked, peeled prawns or diced chicken

1 x 400 g (14 oz) can chopped tomatoes

150 ml (5 fl oz) chicken stock

2 tablespoons chopped fresh parsley

salt and pepper

1 Heat the oil in a large pan and gently cook the onion, garlic, pepper and Cajun seasoning for 5 minutes until the vegetables have softened.

2 Stir in the rice, chorizo, prawns or chicken, tomatoes and stock. Bring to the boil, cover and simmer for 20 minutes until the grains are tender and the liquid has been absorbed, adding more stock if necessary.

3 Stir in the parsley, season to taste and serve.

TIP

Chorizo is a Spanish-style cured sausage with a lovely smoky flavour – it is widely available in supermarkets, but can be substituted with other cured sausages, such as salami.

Creamybaconand sweetcornrisotto

This is not a traditional Italian-style risotto, but a modern British version — it tastes great and is cheap to make, too!

 Preparation: 5 minutes | Cooking time: 25 minutes **Serves 2**

25 g (1 oz) butter

1 small onion, finely chopped

1 large garlic clove

6 rashers smoked streaky bacon, cut widthways into thin strips

225 g (8 oz) risotto rice

600 ml (1 pint) hot chicken stock

1 x 340 g (11¾ oz) can creamed sweetcorn

1 x 150 ml (5 fl oz) carton single cream

2 tablespoons freshly grated Parmesan

salt and pepper

1 Heat the butter in a large pan and gently cook the onion, garlic and bacon for 1–2 minutes.

2 Stir in the rice and cook for 1 minute, stirring continuously until the rice turns opaque. Ladle in a quarter of the stock, stirring until the liquid has been absorbed. Continue to add the stock gradually, stirring occasionally.

3 Stir the sweetcorn and cream into the risotto. Season to taste and warm through gently.

4 Stir a handful of Parmesan into the risotto. Spoon the risotto into a large serving bowl, sprinkle over the remaining Parmesan and serve.

FuManchu friedrice

This beats the local take-away hands down! It takes minutes to make and costs a fraction of the price.

 Preparation: 10 minutes | Cooking time: 15 minutes **Serves 2**

2 tablespoons vegetable oil

2 eggs, beaten

1 x 100 g (4 oz) skinless, boneless chicken breast, roughly chopped

1 garlic clove, finely chopped

2.5 cm (1 in) piece fresh root ginger, finely chopped

1 red pepper, seeded and diced

1 hot Pepperami, thinly sliced

50 g (2 oz) frozen peas, thawed

6 salad onions, thickly sliced

225 g (8 oz) cooked long-grain rice

1 tablespoon soy sauce

1 Heat a little of the oil in a wok or large frying pan. Tip in the beaten eggs and stir with a chopstick until set. Remove from the wok or pan and set aside.

2 Heat the remaining oil in the pan and stir-fry the chicken, garlic, ginger and pepper over a high heat for 5 minutes.

3 Stir in the Pepperami, peas, salad onions, rice and eggs and continue to cook, stirring, for a further 3—4 minutes until piping hot. Season with the soy sauce and serve.

WON'T COOK

Noodle omelette (V)

Instant noodles can be bought from any large grocer's, but if you have difficulty getting hold of them, just cook regular egg noodles in a pan of vegetable stock.

 Preparation: 5 minutes | Cooking time: 10 minutes **Serves 1**

1 x 75 g (3 oz) pack vegetable-flavoured noodles

2 salad onions

1 garlic clove

1 tablespoon vegetable oil

25 g (1 oz) frozen peas, thawed

3 eggs

1 teaspoon soy sauce

salt and pepper

salad and sweet chilli sauce or tomato ketchup, to serve

1 Cook the noodles according to packet instructions; drain well. Meanwhile, thinly slice the salad onions and garlic.

2 Heat the oil in a frying pan and stir-fry the noodles, salad onions, garlic and peas for 2–3 minutes until the noodles begin to brown a little. Season to taste.

3 Meanwhile, beat together the eggs, soy sauce and 2 tablespoons of water. Pour the eggs over the noodle mixture and cook for 2–3 minutes until golden. Carefully flip the omelette and cook for a further minute or two.

4 Slide on to a plate and serve with a dollop of sweet chilli sauce or ketchup and a crisp green salad.

Tropical noodles

Cashew nuts are a bit pricey, but you only need to buy a very small packet — or you can swap them for salted peanuts.

Preparation: 10 minutes | Cooking time: 10 minutes **Serves 2**

100 g (4 oz) Chinese-style egg noodles

1 x 200 g (7 oz) can pineapple chunks in natural juice

1 tablespoon vegetable oil

1 garlic clove, finely chopped

1 bunch of salad onions, thickly sliced on the diagonal

1 large red pepper, seeded and cut into 2 cm (³/4 in) pieces

2 tablespoons sweet chilli sauce

1 tablespoon soy sauce

25 g (1 oz) salted cashew nuts

1 Cook the noodles according to packet instructions. Drain the pineapple chunks, reserving the juice.

2 Meanwhile, heat the oil in a wok or large frying pan, add the pineapple, garlic, salad onions and red pepper and stir-fry over a high heat for 5 minutes until golden and beginning to brown.

3 Stir in the sweet chilli sauce, soy sauce and 2 tablespoons of the reserved pineapple juice. Cook, stirring, for a further 2 minutes until piping hot.

4 Drain the noodles and divide between two plates. Spoon the tropical stir-fry on to the noodles and sprinkle with the cashews. Serve immediately.

TIP

If you don't have any sweet chilli sauce, just stir a little regular chilli sauce into some ketchup.

WON'T
COOK

Hotandsour noodles

The combination of sweet and sour is what gives this dish its lovely flavour. Although brown sugar has a very particular taste that works well here, you can use any type of sugar or even clear honey; you can also swap the white wine vinegar for another kind of 'sour', such as lemon or lime juice or other types of mild vinegar – for example, cider vinegar. Vegetarians can skip the prawns and chicken and add extra vegetables such as salad onions, broccoli and sliced pepper.

 Preparation: 10 minutes | Cooking time: 15 minutes **Serves 2**

100 g (4 oz) Chinese-style egg noodles

300 ml (10 fl oz) hot vegetable stock

2 garlic cloves, finely chopped

1 fresh red chilli, seeded and finely chopped

2.5 cm (1 in) piece root ginger, finely chopped

75 g (3 oz) button mushrooms, thinly sliced

10 raw, peeled tiger prawns or 1 x 100 g (4 oz) skinless, boneless chicken breast, cut into strips

25 g (1 oz) frozen peas, thawed

1 teaspoon brown sugar

1–2 tablespoons soy sauce

1 tablespoon white wine vinegar

2 tablespoons chopped fresh coriander

1 Cook the noodles in a large pan of boiling water according to packet instructions. Drain well and divide between two serving bowls.

2 Meanwhile, place the stock, garlic, chilli and ginger in a small pan and bring to the boil. Add the mushrooms and prawns or chicken and simmer gently for 10 minutes.

3 Stir in the peas, sugar, soy sauce and vinegar and simmer for a further minute or so until the vegetables are tender. Ladle the mixture over the noodles, scatter over the coriander and serve.

Satay chickennoodles

Coconut cream is a great ingredient when making Thai-style dishes. It comes in handy 200 ml (7 fl oz) cartons from most supermarkets and isn't too expensive.

 Preparation: 10 minutes | Cooking time: 10 minutes **Serves 2**

150 g (5 oz) rice noodles

vegetable oil, for frying

2 chicken breasts, cut into 1 cm (1/2 in) wide strips

250 g (9 oz) mixed vegetables, e.g. carrots, broccoli, mangetout, corn, bean sprouts, sliced if large

For the satay sauce

100 g (4 oz) dry-roasted peanuts

1 garlic clove, crushed

1 x 200 ml (7 fl oz) carton coconut cream

1 tablespoon soy sauce

juice of 1 lime

1 Make the sauce: place the peanuts in a plastic bag and crush with a rolling pin or similar. Save a handful to sprinkle over the top and place the remainder in a bowl with the garlic, coconut cream, soy sauce and lime juice. Mix well together.

2 Cook the noodles in a large pan of boiling water for 2—3 minutes according to packet instructions.

3 Heat a little oil in a wok or large frying pan and stir-fry the chicken over a high heat for 3 minutes.

4 Drain the noodles and cool under cold water. Turn into a colander and set aside to drain.

5 Add the vegetables to the wok and cook for a further minute. Stir in the satay sauce and cook for 1—2 minutes until piping hot.

6 Stir the cooked noodles into the wok, then transfer to two large bowls, sprinkle over the reserved, crushed nuts and serve immediately.

WON'T
COOK

Kingprawn chowmein

This is a bit on the extravagant side, but you can always use cubes of pork or chicken in place of the prawns — just ensure they are fully cooked through before you serve. The cornflour gives the dish a glossy, slightly thickened finish — if you don't have any, just leave it out and don't use the water that's added during the last step.

 Preparation: 5 minutes | Cooking time: 10 minutes **Serves 2**

100 g (4 oz) Chinese-style egg noodles

12 raw king prawns, peeled

1—2 teaspoons cornflour

1 tablespoon vegetable oil

1 onion, thinly sliced

1 garlic clove, thinly sliced

50 g (2 oz) frozen peas, thawed

100 g (4 oz) bean sprouts

3 tablespoons soy sauce

1 tablespoon chilli sauce

salt and pepper

1 Plunge the noodles into a large pan of boiling water and cook for 3—4 minutes or according to the packet instructions. Meanwile, dust the king prawns with the cornflour.

2 Heat the vegetable oil in a wok and stir-fry the onion and garlic over a high heat for 1 minute. Add the prawns and cook for a further minute until the prawns become pink.

3 Drain the noodles and add to the wok with the peas and bean sprouts and cook for a further minute.

4 Stir together the soy sauce and chilli sauce and pour into the wok. Stir in 3—4 tablespoons of water and bubble together for 1—2 minutes until the mixture is piping hot. Season to taste and serve.

Crispychickenthighs

If you can't find boneless chicken thighs that still have their skin on in supermarkets, ask your local butcher to bone out the whole chicken thighs for you.

 Preparation: 15 minutes | Cooking time: 20 minutes **Serves 2**

2 garlic cloves, finely chopped

1 fresh red chilli, seeded and finely chopped, or 1/4 teaspoon dried chilli flakes

grated rind and juice of 1 lemon

2 tablespoons chopped fresh coriander or parsley

4 boneless chicken thighs with skin

salt and pepper

boiled Thai fragrant or basmati rice and green vegetables such as broccoli, to serve

1 Mix together the garlic, chilli, lemon rind and coriander or parsley. Generously season the chicken thighs, then gently loosen the skin from the flesh. Spoon the chilli mixture between the skin and the flesh, then stretch the skin back into place.

2 Heat a large non-stick frying pan and cook the chicken thighs skin-side down for 20 minutes over a medium heat, without turning, until the skin is crunchy and deep golden and the flesh has cooked through.

3 Turn the chicken and squeeze over the lemon juice. Cook for a further minute or so, then serve skin-side up with plain rice and green vegetables.

Porknoodlesoup

This really easy yet very filling soup can also be made with chicken or beef — buy the stir-fry strips if you're short on time. Pak choi is a crisp, green Chinese vegetable increasingly available in grocers and supermarkets.

 Preparation: 10 minutes | Cooking time: 10 minutes **Serves 2**

100 g (4 oz) rice noodles

1 tablespoon vegetable oil

150 g (5 oz) lean pork fillet, cut into 1 cm (½ in) wide strips

600 ml (1 pint) hot chicken stock

1 tablespoon Thai red curry paste

200 g (7 oz) pak choi or spinach

4 salad onions, finely chopped

2 tablespoons soy sauce

juice of 1/2 lemon

1 Cook the noodles in a large pan of boiling water according to packet instructions. Drain well.

2 Heat the oil in a large pan and cook the pork over a high heat for 2–3 minutes, stirring until well browned. Add the hot stock and curry paste, bring to the boil and simmer for 5 minutes.

3 Stir in the greens and salad onions and cook for 1–2 minutes, then add the soy sauce and lemon juice.

4 Divide the noodles between two bowls and pour over the hot soup. Serve immediately.

WON'T
COOK

Stir-fried vegetablesoba Ⓥ

Soba noodles are made from buckwheat flour and have a lovely nutty flavour. They can be bought from large supermarkets or health-food shops, but you can always use regular Chinese-style egg noodles for this dish if you have difficulty getting hold of soba noodles.

 Preparation: 10 minutes | Cooking time: 10 minutes **Serves 2**

150 g (5 oz) soba noodles

1 tablespoon vegetable oil

2.5 cm (1 in) piece root ginger, finely chopped

1 garlic clove, finely chopped

1 large carrot, cut into matchsticks

100 g (4 oz) mangetout or frozen peas, thawed

100 g (4 oz) button mushrooms, halved

1 egg, beaten

2 salad onions, finely chopped

2 tablespoons soy sauce

1 teaspoon vinegar

salt and pepper

1 Cook the noodles in a large pan of boiling water according to packet instructions. Drain well, then cool under cold water.

2 Heat the oil in a wok or large frying pan and stir-fry the ginger, garlic, carrot, mangetout or peas and mushrooms over a high heat for 2–3 minutes until golden.

3 Add the cooked noodles, beaten egg and salad onions and stir-fry for 1–2 minutes until the egg has set.

4 Stir in the soy sauce and vinegar and season to taste. Divide between two plates and serve immediately.

Kedgeree

This classic breakfast dish is great served any time of day. Kippers might be a bit stinky, but if you stick to the boil-in-the-bag type, you'll minimize the smell.

 Preparation: 5 minutes | Cooking time: 20 minutes **Serves 2**

225 g (8 oz) long-grain rice

1 x 230 g (8½ oz) pack boil-in-the-bag kippers

2 eggs

4 tablespoons single cream (optional)

1 tablespoon roughly chopped fresh parsley

salt and pepper

1 Cook the rice in a large pan of boiling, salted water, without stirring, for 15 minutes until tender. Meanwhile, place the bag of kippers and the eggs in second pan of boiling water and cook for 8 minutes.

2 Remove the kippers from the pan and set aside. Cool the eggs under running water, then shell and roughly chop them. Drain the rice.

3 Open the packet of kippers with a pair of scissors and carefully tip the butter and juices inside the packet into a large frying pan. Roughly flake the fish and add to the pan with the rice, eggs and cream, if using. Heat gently together for 2–3 minutes, then stir in the parsley. Season to taste and serve.

Carrotcakes

No, not the sweet kind, but delicious little fritters that make the most of left-over rice. Try substituting the coriander for other soft herbs such as parsley, chives or basil.

 Preparation: 10 minutes | Cooking time: 10 minutes **Serves 2**

175 g (6 oz) cooked long-grain rice

2 carrots, grated

50 g (2 oz) grated Cheddar

2 garlic cloves, crushed

2 tablespoons chopped fresh coriander

3 tablespoons flour

1 egg, beaten

2 tablespoons vegetable oil

salt and pepper

baked beans, to serve

1 Stir together the rice, carrots, cheese, garlic, coriander, 1–2 tablespoons of flour, the egg and plenty of seasoning. Firmly shape into six even-sized cakes, then dust with a little more flour.

2 Heat the oil in large frying pan and cook the cakes for 3–4 minutes on each side until golden brown.

3 Drain on kitchen paper and serve with baked beans.

WON'T
COOK

curries and stews

Moroccan-style chickenstew

This delicious, soupy style of stew is served with couscous, which absorbs all the flavour and juices of the stew. It is a very good dish for making ahead and re-heating the following day.

 Preparation: 10 minutes | Cooking time: 30 minutes **Serves 2**

150 g (5 oz) couscous

200 ml (7 fl oz) chicken stock

For the chicken stew

1/2 teaspoon mixed spice

1/2 teaspoon salt

4 x 75 g (3 oz) skinless, boneless chicken thighs

1 tablespoon sunflower oil

300 ml (10 fl oz) hot chicken stock

2 garlic cloves, thinly sliced

juice of 1 lemon

2 tomatoes, roughly chopped

50 g (2 oz) black olives

2 tablespoons chopped fresh coriander (optional)

salt and pepper

hot chilli sauce, to serve

1 Place the couscous in a large bowl and pour over the 200ml (7 fl oz) hot chicken stock; set aside for the grains to absorb the liquid, stirring occasionally.

2 Mix together the spice and salt and sprinkle over the chicken. Heat the oil in large pan and cook the chicken for 2—3 minutes on each side until golden brown.

3 Stir in the 300ml (10 fl oz) hot chicken stock, garlic, lemon juice, tomatoes and olives and simmer gently for 20 minutes until the chicken is cooked through. Season to taste and stir in the coriander, if using.

4 Divide the couscous between two bowls and spoon over the chicken stew. Top each bowl with a splash of the chilli sauce and eat immediately.

WON'T
COOK

Sweetchickpeastew (V)

This a lovely Turkish-style stew. Serve with crusty bread for a thoroughly warming supper.

 Preparation: 10 minutes | Cooking time: 20 minutes **Serves 2**

2 tablespoons sunflower oil

1 onion, finely chopped

1 sweet potato, diced

1 garlic clove, thinly sliced

1 x 400 g (14 oz) can chick peas, drained

2 tomatoes, roughly chopped

1 teaspoon honey

300 ml (10 fl oz) hot vegetable stock

250 g (9 oz) fresh spinach

salt and pepper

warm crusty bread, to serve

1 Heat the oil in a large pan and cook the onion, sweet potato and garlic for 5 minutes, stirring until beginning to soften and brown. Stir in the chick peas, tomatoes and honey and cook for 1—2 minutes until the tomatoes begin to soften.

2 Stir in the hot stock, bring to the boil, then cover and simmer for 10 minutes until the sweet potato is tender.

3 Stir in the spinach and cook for 1 minute, stirring until the spinach wilts. Season to taste, ladle into large bowls and serve with crusty bread to mop up the juices.

Beefinredwine

This recipe uses quite a cheap cut of meat so it does take longer than the average dish to cook. However, the result really is quite smart — ideal for entertaining.

 Preparation: 10 minutes | Cooking time: 1 hour **Serves 2**

1—2 tablespoons olive oil

250 g (9 oz) braising or stewing steak, cubed

1 tablespoon flour, seasoned with salt and pepper

1 onion, finely chopped

1 garlic clove

75 g (3 oz) smoked streaky bacon, roughly chopped

200 ml (7 fl oz) red wine

1/4 teaspoon dried thyme or sage

salt and pepper

mashed potatoes and steamed greens, to serve

1 Heat the oil in large pan. Dust the beef with seasoned flour and cook in the pan for 1—2 minutes until beginning to brown.

2 Add the onion, garlic and bacon and cook for a further 1—2 minutes until beginning to brown. Stir in the wine and herbs, bring to the boil, cover and simmer for 1 hour. Season to taste and serve with mashed potatoes and greens.

TIP

Turn this dish into a simple Coq au Vin. Swap the steak for skinless chicken thighs, add some button mushrooms with the onion and cut the cooking time down to 30 minutes.

Tandoorichicken

Okay, so it's not strictly a curry, but a good tandoori chicken goes down well with all the usual Indian-style trimmings. To make it properly, however, you are going to need a few authentic spices.

 Preparation: 10 minutes | Cooking time: 30 minutes **Serves 2**

1 x 150 g (5 oz) carton natural yogurt

2 garlic cloves, crushed

1 teaspoon ground cumin

1/2 teaspoon chilli powder

1/4 teaspoon ground turmeric

a few drops of red food colouring

2 medium chicken quarters

salt and pepper

cucumber raita and lemon wedges, to serve

1 Pre-heat the oven to 200°C/400°F/Gas 6.

2 In a large, shallow dish, stir together the yogurt, garlic, cumin, chilli, turmeric, food colouring and plenty of salt and pepper.

3 Toss the chicken quarters in the mixture until well coated. Place on a baking sheet and roast for 30 minutes until completely cooked through.

4 Serve with cucumber raita and lemon wedges.

Rustic lamb and beans

This is quite a posh dish, but it really is easy to make.

 Preparation: 5 minutes | Cooking time: 15 minutes **Serves 2**

2 tablespoons olive oil

1 onion, finely chopped

2 garlic cloves, finely chopped

4 rashers smoked streaky bacon, cut into small strips

150 ml (5 fl oz) red wine

6 medium lamb chops

1 x 400 g (14 oz) can cannellini beans, drained

1 x 400 g (14 oz) can chopped tomatoes

2 teaspoons chopped fresh rosemary or 1 teaspoon dried

1 tablespoon tomato ketchup

a pinch of dried chilli flakes

salt and pepper

1 Heat 1 tablespoon of oil in a pan and cook the onion, garlic and bacon for 5 minutes until well browned. Pour in the wine, stirring with a wooden spoon to scrape up any residue; bring to the boil and simmer for 5 minutes.

2 Meanwhile, heat the remaining tablespoon of olive oil in a frying pan and cook the lamb for 6 minutes, turning once until well browned but still a little pink in the centre.

3 Stir the beans, tomatoes, rosemary, ketchup and chilli flakes into the bacon pan. Bring to the boil and simmer for 5 minutes; season to taste.

4 Spoon the beans into large bowls and top with the lamb chops.

Redroastlamb

*This is incredibly easy to make, yet tastes like it takes a whole load of effort.
A great dish for entertaining.*

 Preparation: 10 minutes | Cooking time: 1 hour **Serves 2**

300 g (10 oz) piece lamb neck fillet, cut
into bite-sized pieces

150 ml (5 fl oz) red wine

4 tomatoes, quartered

4 garlic cloves

4 rosemary sprigs

salt and pepper

Turkish-style flat bread and salad, to serve

1 Pre-heat the oven to 200°C/400°F/Gas 6.

2 Place the lamb in a small roasting tin with the
wine, tomatoes, garlic, rosemary and plenty of
seasoning. Roast for 1 hour, turning occasionally.

3 Serve with flat bread and leafy salad.

Sausagehot-pot

*This is a really tasty supper dish — if you have an extra few minutes to spare,
place the finished dish under a hot grill until the cheese is melted and bubbling.*

 Preparation: 5 minutes | Cooking time: 20 minutes **Serves 2**

2 tablespoons vegetable oil

225 g (8 oz) spicy chipolata sausages

1 large onion, roughly chopped

1 large potato, diced

1 garlic clove thinly sliced

300 ml (10 fl oz) hot chicken stock

1 x 400 g (14 oz) can baked beans

50 g (2 oz) Cheddar, grated

salt and pepper

1 Heat 1 tablespoon of the oil in a large pan and
cook the sausages for 5 minutes until well browned.
Remove from the pan and set aside.

2 Add the remaining oil, the onion, potato and
garlic to the pan and cook for 3–4 minutes, stirring
until beginning to brown.

3 Pour in the stock and return the sausages to the
pan. Bring to the boil, cover and simmer for 10
minutes until the sausages are cooked through and
the potato is tender.

4 Stir in the baked beans and cook for 2–3
minutes until warmed through; season to taste.
Spoon the hot-pot into serving bowls, sprinkle over
the cheese and serve.

CAN'T
COOK

Quicklambbiryani

Lamb neck fillet is a great cut of meat for this kind of dish — it's cheap to buy, is not too lean and yet is still nice and tender.

 Preparation: 10 minutes | Cooking time: 20 minutes **Serves 2**

25 g (1 oz) butter

1 large onion, thinly sliced

1 tablespoon curry paste

1 teaspoon cornflour

1 x 150 g (5 oz) carton natural yoghurt

1 onion, grated

2 garlic cloves, crushed

1/2 teaspoon salt

250 g (9 oz) lamb neck fillet, cubed

150 g (5 oz) basmati rice

1 egg

salt and pepper

1 Heat the butter in a large frying pan and gently cook the sliced onion for 10 minutes until golden.

2 In a large bowl, mix together the curry paste, cornflour, yoghurt, grated onion, garlic, salt and lamb.

3 Cook the rice in a large pan of boiling, salted water for 10 minutes until tender. Boil the egg in a separate pan of water for 8 minutes.

4 Remove a spoonful of the golden onions from the frying pan and set aside. Add the lamb mixture to the hot pan with 100 ml (3 1/2 fl oz) of water and simmer together for 5–6 minutes; season to taste.

5 Drain the egg, place under running water until cool enough to handle. Shell the egg and cut into quarters.

6 Drain the rice and stir into the lamb pan; cook for 1–2 minutes then spoon on to two plates. Top each serving with a couple of egg wedges and some of the reserved golden onions.

WON'T
COOK

Chicken balti

For a satisfying supper, serve your chicken balti with some warmed naan and a glass of cold lager.

 Preparation: 5 minutes | Cooking time: 20 minutes **Serves 2**

1 tablespoon vegetable oil

300 g (11 oz) boneless, skinless chicken, cubed

1 onion, finely chopped

3 garlic cloves, finely chopped

2.5 cm (1 in) piece root ginger, grated

4 tomatoes, roughly chopped

3–4 tablespoons balti curry paste

1 teaspoon cornflour

juice of ½ lemon

1 x 150 g (5 oz) carton Greek-style yoghurt

4 tablespoons chopped fresh coriander (optional)

salt and pepper

1 Heat the oil in a large frying pan and stir-fry the chicken, onion, garlic and ginger for 3 minutes.

2 Add the tomatoes, curry paste and 3–4 tablespoons of water and cook gently for 10 minutes, stirring occasionally until the chicken is cooked.

3 Dissolve the cornflour in the lemon juice, then stir into the yoghurt with the coriander, if using. Add the yoghurt mixture to the balti and heat through gently; season to taste and serve.

Spicy dhal

Dhal is a lovely soft curry made from lentils. Serve it with rice or naan bread for a complete meal.

 Preparation: 5 minutes | Cooking time: 20 minutes **Serves 2**

1 tablespoon sunflower oil

2.5 cm (1 in) piece fresh root ginger, very finely chopped

1 small onion, finely chopped

2 garlic cloves, finely chopped

150 g (5 oz) dried red lentils

600 ml (1 pint) hot vegetable stock

1 tablespoon hot curry paste

juice of ½ lemon

a handful of fresh coriander leaves, roughly chopped (optional)

salt and pepper

1 Heat the oil in a large pan and cook the ginger, onion and garlic for 5 minutes until softened and golden.

2 Stir in the lentils, stock and curry paste. Bring to the boil, cover and cook gently for 15 minutes, stirring occasionally until the lentils are tender and the mixture is thick.

3 Stir in the lemon juice with the coriander, if using; season to taste and serve.

Egg curry

Not the most appetizing name for a dish, but this really does taste a heck of a lot better than it sounds ...

 Preparation: 15 minutes | Cooking time: 20 minutes **Serves 2**

4 eggs

4 tablespoons sunflower oil

1 onion, thinly sliced

1 onion, grated

2.5 cm (1 in) piece root ginger, grated

2 garlic cloves, crushed

1 tablespoon curry paste

4 tomatoes, roughly chopped

1 x 150 ml (5 fl oz) carton double cream

2 tablespoons chopped fresh coriander (optional)

salt and pepper

boiled rice, to serve

1 Cook the eggs in a pan of boiling water for 10 minutes.

2 Heat the oil in a heavy-based frying pan and cook the sliced onions for 3–4 minutes until crisp and well browned; drain on kitchen paper and set aside.

3 Cook the grated onion, ginger and garlic in the same pan for 2–3 minutes until beginning to soften. Stir in the curry paste and tomatoes; season well and cook for 2–3 minutes, stirring until the tomatoes begin to soften.

4 Stir in the cream and 100 ml (3½ fl oz) of water. Bring to the boil and simmer for 2–3 minutes.

5 Drain the eggs, cool under cold water, then shell and halve them. Roughly chop the crispy onions and stir into the pan with the eggs and coriander. Simmer gently for 5 minutes; season to taste and serve with rice.

Meatball curry

This dish hails from Kashmir in northern India, which is where most of the creamy-style curries such as the korma originate. It is quite mild and is lovely served with plain, boiled basmati rice and a spoonful of fruit chutney.

 Preparation: 5 minutes | Cooking time: 15 minutes **Serves 2**

250 g (9 oz) lean minced chicken or turkey

2 garlic cloves, crushed

1/2 teaspoon dried chilli flakes

2 tablespoons sunflower oil

1 onion, finely chopped

50 g (2 oz) ground almonds

1 x 150 ml (5 fl oz) carton double cream

150 ml (5 fl oz) milk

1 tablespoon medium curry paste

2 tablespoons chopped fresh coriander

salt and pepper

1 Mix together the chicken or turkey, garlic and chilli, then shape into 6–8 small balls.

2 Heat the oil in a pan and cook the onion and ground almonds for 5 minutes, stirring continuously until golden brown. Stir in the cream, milk and curry paste and gently bring to a simmer. Add the meatballs, cover and simmer for 10 minutes, stirring occasionally until the meatballs are cooked.

3 Stir in the coriander and season to taste.

Creole
shrimpcurry

Don't let the seeding and slicing of chillies put you off — this is a very tasty curry that's well worth the effort.

 Preparation: 10 minutes | Cooking time: 15 minutes **Serves 2**

200 g (7 oz) cooked, peeled prawns

1 tablespoon vinegar

1 teaspoon sugar

1/2 teaspoon salt

4 garlic cloves, crushed

6 fresh green chillies, seeded and thinly sliced

1 tablespoon sunflower oil

1 onion, finely chopped

1 tablespoon curry paste

250 ml (8 fl oz) tomato juice

1 x 180 g (6 3/4 oz) can sweetcorn, drained

salt and pepper

naan bread or boiled rice, to serve

1 Place the prawns, vinegar, sugar, salt, garlic and chillies in a bowl, mix well together and set aside to marinate for 5—10 minutes.

2 Heat the oil in a wok or large frying pan and cook the onion over a high heat for 3—4 minutes until lightly browned; add the prawn mixture and stir-fry for a further 2 minutes.

3 Stir in the curry paste, tomato juice and sweetcorn. Bring to the boil and simmer for 5 minutes. Season to taste and serve with naan bread or rice.

Thai-style fishcurry

This fashionable dish is much easier to make than you may think — a good choice if you're out to impress.

 Preparation: 5 minutes | Cooking time: 15 minutes **Serves 2**

1 tablespoon sunflower oil

1 small onion, thinly sliced

2 tomatoes, roughly diced

1 x 200 g (7 oz) carton coconut cream

1 tablespoon Thai red curry paste

250 g (9 oz) cubed, skinned white fish such as cod, haddock or coley

juice of 1 lime

1 tablespoon soy sauce

a handful of fresh basil leaves

salt and pepper

cooked rice and steamed sugar-snap peas or mangetout, to serve

1 Heat the oil in a large, non-stick pan and cook the onion over a high heat for 4—5 minutes until beginning to brown.

2 Add the tomatoes and cook for 1 minute, then stir in the coconut cream and curry paste. Bring to a gentle simmer and add the fish; cook gently for 4—5 minutes until the fish is just tender.

3 Stir in the lime juice, soy sauce and basil and season to taste. Spoon the rice into serving bowls and gently ladle over the fish curry; serve with sugar-snap peas or mangetout.

puddings

Baked marzipan peaches

Quite a stylish dessert this — make it in the summer when the peaches are cheap and at their best.

 Preparation: 15 minutes | Cooking time: 15 minutes **Serves 2**

100 g (4 oz) white marzipan, chilled

25 g (1 oz) flaked almonds

3 peaches

a knob of butter

2 tablespoons demerara sugar

4 tablespoons dark rum or whisky

ice cream, to serve

1 Pre-heat the oven to 200°C/400°F/Gas 6. Cut the marzipan into 5 mm (¼ in) dice and mix with the flaked almonds.

2 Halve the peaches, remove the stones and arrange in a buttered ovenproof dish. Spoon the marzipan mixture into the hollows, piling the mixture high. Sprinkle over the demerara sugar and bake for 5 minutes.

3 Remove the peaches from the oven and pour in the rum. Return to the oven and cook for a further 8 minutes until the marzipan is melted and golden brown and the peaches are tender.

4 Place three peach halves on each plate and top with a large scoop of vanilla ice cream; serve immediately.

Bitterchocpots

Choose good-quality dark chocolate with a minimum of 50 per cent cocoa solids for this dessert. If the mixture stiffens before it has been well blended, either beat in a couple of tablespoons of boiling water or pop into a microwave for 5–10 seconds.

 Preparation: 10 minutes | Cooling time: 15 minutes **Serves 2**

100 g (4 oz) dark chocolate

1 x 200 g (7oz) carton fromage frais

2 tablespoons icing sugar

1 Break the chocolate into a small heatproof bowl. Sit the bowl over a pan of gently simmering water and leave for 2–3 minutes until the chocolate melts.

2 Quickly beat in the fromage frais and icing sugar to taste. Spoon the mixture into small cups or glasses and chill for at least 15 minutes until cool and set.

Ginandlimefroth

This can be made with gin or without any alcohol at all. It is also very good when frozen for an hour or so – perfect for cooling down on a hot summer's day.

 Preparation: 10 minutes | Cooling time: 2 hours **Serves 4**

1 x 135 g (4³/₄ oz) packet lime or lemon jelly

4 tablespoons gin

1 x 200 g (7 oz) carton Greek-style yoghurt

1 Dissolve the jelly in 300 ml (10 fl oz) of boiling water, stirring occasionally; set aside to cool.

2 Once the mixture is cool but before the jelly has begun to set, whisk in the gin, if using, and yoghurt until frothy and well blended.

3 Pour the mixture into small glasses and leave to set in the fridge.

Pineapplefritters

Try this with other fruit such as banana or apple.

 Preparation: 5 minutes | Cooking time: 5 minutes **Serves 2**

1 egg

2 tablespoons milk

1 tablespoon caster sugar

50 g (2 oz) self-raising flour, plus extra for dusting

1 x 200 g (7 oz) can pineapple rings, drained

sunflower oil, for frying

ice cream, to serve

1 Crack the egg into a bowl and whisk in the milk, sugar and flour.

2 Heat 5 cm (2 in) of sunflower oil in a small, deep pan.

3 Dust the pineapple rings in a little flour, then dip in the batter. Cook in the hot oil for 3—4 minutes until crisp and golden. Serve immediately with a scoop of vanilla ice cream.

Apricotcustardcrumble

This a lovely, warming pudding. Don't worry if the custard bubbles up around the edges a little, it won't spoil the flavour.

 Preparation: 10 minutes | Cooking time: 25 minutes **Serves 2—3**

100 g (4 oz) plain flour

50 g (2 oz) butter, diced

50 g (2 oz) caster sugar

a pinch of ground ginger (optional)

1 x 150 g (5 oz) carton custard

1 x 400 g (14 oz) can apricot halves in natural juice

1 Pre-heat the oven to 190°C/375°F/Gas 5.

2 Place the flour in a bowl and rub in the butter with your fingertips until it resembles fine breadcrumbs. Stir in the caster sugar and ginger, if using.

3 Pour the custard into the base of a small ovenproof dish, then carefully spoon over the apricot halves and 2—3 tablespoons of the juice.

4 Sprinkle over the crumble topping and bake for 20—25 minutes until golden brown. Serve warm.

WON'T
COOK

Honeyed basmati rice pudding

This is a speedy version of the classic comfort pudding. Try adding flavourings of your choice, such as raisins or grated orange rind, if you wish.

 Preparation: 2 minutes | Cooking time: 15 minutes **Serves 2**

450 ml (15 fl oz) milk
___

3 tablespoons clear honey
___

a few drops of vanilla extract
___

150 g (5 oz) basmati rice

1 Place the milk, honey and vanilla extract in a pan and bring to the boil.

2 Stir in the basmati rice, cover and simmer for 15 minutes, stirring occasionally, until the grains are tender.

Snappy cheesecakes

Brandy-snap baskets can be bought from most supermarkets and just need filling for a really speedy dessert. Try them with ice cream and sliced fruit, chocolate mousse or fruit compote and yoghurt.

 Preparation: 5 minutes **Serves 2**

100 g (4 oz) mascarpone
___

2 tablespoons lemon curd
___

4 brandy-snap baskets
___

1 flaky chocolate bar

1 Beat together the mascarpone and lemon curd and spoon into the brandy-snap baskets.

2 Crumble over the chocolate and serve.

Classiccitruspancakes

Pancakes can be served with lots of different toppings — try frying slices of banana in butter, or topping them with ice cream, melted chocolate or fruity fromage frais.

 Preparation: 5 minutes | Cooking time: 10 minutes **Serves 2**

100 g (4 oz) plain flour

a pinch of salt

1 egg

300 ml (10 fl oz) milk

sunflower oil, for frying

sugar and oranges or lemons, to serve

1 Place the flour and salt in large bowl and make a well in the centre. Beat together the egg and milk, then gradually whisk into the flour to make a smooth batter.

2 Heat a little oil in a frying pan and when the pan is hot pour in just enough batter, swirling to coat the base thinly. Cook for 1 minute until golden, then flip and cook the second side for 30 seconds.

3 Continue to make more pancakes in the same way, then sprinkle over a little sugar and a squeeze of orange or lemon juice; serve warm.

Lemonposset

This a truly fantastic pudding — the acid in the lemon sets the warm cream so it becomes a soft cheese.

 Preparation: 5 minutes | Cooling time: 30 minutes **Serves 2**

1 x 300 ml (10 fl oz) carton double cream

75 g (3 oz) caster sugar

grated rind and juice of 1 lemon

chocolate biscuits, to serve

1 Place the cream and sugar in pan and bring to the boil, stirring until the sugar dissolves.

2 Add the lemon juice and stir until thickened, then pour into glasses; chill until the mixture has set. Serve with chocolate biscuits.

Speedycrèmebrûlée

Crème brûlées traditionally take hours to make. This cheat's version is ready in a flash and the result is truly impressive.

 Preparation: 10 minutes | Cooking time: 5 minutes **Serves 4**

grated rind of 1 large orange

1 x 250 g (9 oz) carton mascarpone

1 x 400 g (14 oz) carton fresh custard

6 tablespoons caster sugar

small jar fruit compote, e.g. apricot or cherry

1 Pre-heat the grill to high. Mix together the orange rind and mascarpone. Gradually add the custard, beating until smooth and thick.

2 Spoon 2 tablespoons of compote into the bottom of each of four ramekins or heatproof teacups and top with the custard mixture.

3 Level the top of the custard and sprinkle over a thick layer of caster sugar.

4 Place the ramekins under the grill and cook for 2–3 minutes until the sugar melts and turns dark golden. Serve immediately.

Stickytoffeepudding

This is another short-cut pud, but it really works a treat.

 Preparation: 5 minutes | Cooking time: 10 minutes **Serves 2**

50 g (2 oz) butter

100 g (4 oz) brown sugar

1 x 150 ml (5 fl oz) carton double cream

200 g (7 oz) Madeira cake

a knob of butter

custard, to serve

1 Pre-heat the oven to 190°C/375°F/Gas 5. Place the butter, sugar and cream in a small pan and heat gently, stirring, until the mixture is well blended.

2 Roughly crumble the cake into a small, buttered, ovenproof dish. Pour over the sauce and cook in the oven for 10 minutes until bubbling. Spoon into bowls and serve with custard.

Index

WON'T COOK

Index contd.

CAN'T
COOK